*Praise for*
# Love in Action

A thought-provoking challenge to all of us who love the Catholic Church and believe in the power of nonviolence.

> —MARIE DENNIS, Maryknoll Office for Global Concerns

An ancient axiom tells us that "our Church is always in need of reform [*Ecclesia semper reformada*]". What better way to bring about reform than through the "active love" (nonviolence) modeled by Jesus? *Love in Action* teaches us to do just that.

> —BISHOP THOMAS J. GUMBLETON, Detroit, Mich.

Nearly all of us understand the meaning of love. Many of us understand the meaning of "tough love." But do we understand the importance of love united with action? Richard Taylor helps us turn our love of Catholic faith and gospel values into "love in action." He is first and foremost a teacher, and his lifetime of nonviolent action to secure social justice is inspirational. In this book, he teaches us how to be true to our deepest beliefs in Jesus, in justice, and the gift of using our knowledge and faith to make a difference. Every Catholic can use this book in their daily life. **—JIM POST, Cofounder, Voice of the Faithful**

A common response among dedicated Catholics hoping for a significant reform in the institutional church has been discouragement. Yet the reality is that gospel nonviolence is more powerful than any other force for bringing about radical change in structures that have become encrusted with selfishness and narcissism. This hard-hitting handbook grounds us in the need for persistence and hope. Its goals are real and solidly rooted in the mission of Christ; the methodology is realistic and concrete; and the end result is reachable.

The clergy sexual abuse "crisis" has served as the catalyst to awaken the realization that reform and renewal in the Spirit of Christ is not only needed, but radically essential if Catholic Christians are to remain true to their baptismal calling. *Love in Action* is one result of this crisis. It serves as a handbook for much more than nonviolent methods. It's really a handbook for how to live out one's baptism...

> —THOMAS P. DOYLE, JCD, CADC

This wonderful resource may have been written for just this moment in time. —REA HOWARTH, The Quixote Center

Richard Taylor not only talks the talk, but he has—and does—walk the walk. Drawing on years of experience in prayer and nonviolent direct action, he has constructed a handbook which is invaluable for any group seeking Church reform. "Give it a try," Dick encourages. If we all gave it a try, the reign of God would be very close.

—**GAILE M. POHLHAUS, PHD, retired professor of theology at Villanova University; recipient of the 2007 College Theology Society National Service Award**

The Roman Catholic Church has proclaimed Jesus' powerful vision and practice of transformative love and nonviolence in lives and societies around the world for two thousand years. In *Love in Action*, Richard K. Taylor clearly and comprehensively reveals how this gospel nonviolence can be unleashed to reform the church itself. After exploring how the heart of the Good News is also the heart of spiritually-grounded nonviolence, Taylor carefully lays out the steps and strategies of gospel nonviolence and their application to the contemporary call to help free the church to become—within and without—a new force for justice and peace. Taylor's resource will play an important role in present and future initiatives to create a more inclusive and just Catholic community. —**KEN BUTIGAN, Pace e Bene Nonviolence Service**

I especially appreciate Taylor's emphasis on discernment, preparing spiritually, strategizing and negotiation before moving to nonviolent direct action. Too often people want to picket the cathedral without a plan, or worse without talking to diocesan officials. *Love in Action* contains vitally important tools for building a more effective church reform movement. —**CHRISTINE SCHENK, CSJ, Executive Director of FutureChurch**

Richard Taylor's *Love In Action* is, as its subtitle states: *A Direct-Action Handbook for Catholics Using Gospel Nonviolence to Reform and Renew the Church*. Now there can be no excuse saying, "I wish the Catholic Church would reform and renew itself according to Vatican Council II—but what can I do about it?" *Love In Action* tells us precisely how to do it. What are you waiting for?! —**LEONARD SWIDLER, PHD, Cofounder of the Association for the Rights of Catholics in the Church (ARCC)**

*Love In Action* comes just in the nick of time. I hope it will be read far and wide, studied by Church groups, and put into practice, so that we can all become more nonviolent and loving, and together disarm, heal, and transform our Church into a community of love in action.

—**FR. JOHN DEAR, SJ, author *of Living Peace, Jesus the Rebel, The God of Peace*, and *Transfiguration***

# Love in Action

## A Direct Action Handbook
for Catholics Using Gospel Nonviolence
to Reform and Renew the Church

Richard K. Taylor

*Love In Action: A Direct Action Handbook for Catholics Using Gospel Nonviolence to Reform and Renew the Church*

R. K. Taylor Publishing, Philadelphia 19119
© 2007 by Richard K. Taylor
All rights reserved. Published 2007

ISBN: 978-0-9794369-0-1

Additional copies may be ordered online at www.gospelnonviolence.com or by emailing sales@gospelnonviolence.com. You may also write R. K. Taylor Publishing, 609 E. Allens Lane, Philadelphia, PA 19119.

R. K. Taylor Publishing has made every effort to trace the ownership of all quotes. In the event of a question arising from the use of a quote, we regret any error made and will be pleased to make the necessary correction in future printings and editions of this book.

Bible quotations in this volume are from the New American Bible unless otherwise indicated.

Printed on acid-free and lingin-free paper which meets all ANSI standards for archival quality paper.

Design by Ellen Moore Osborne, www.TrinityArts.com.

Printed in the U.S.A.

First Edition, 2007

# Contents

# Overview

I've written this handbook for those who care deeply about the Catholic Church and who, because of their love, are committed to Church reform and renewal. Its purpose is to help faithful Catholics explore how to use gospel nonviolence in their reform efforts. The approach is termed *gospel nonviolence* because it is rooted in the life, teachings, death, resurrection, and continued guiding presence of Jesus Christ as well as in Church tradition. This phrase also distinguishes it from forms of nonviolence that are not spiritually based and do not make creative love (including *agape* love for opponents) central to their disciplines.

You will find here all you need to know to put together a direct-action campaign based on gospel nonviolence. The table of contents offers a clear outline of all the material in this handbook. Five appendixes cover essential topics in more detail.

If you are an organizer on the run, take a look at Appendix 2, "The Organizer's Checklist." You'll find it an indispensable list of reminders as you work to build a successful, well-organized campaign.

Many scholars and practitioners of nonviolence have written excellent works on the subject, addressing both its tactics and its spiritual and philosophical foundations. This, however, is the only book dedicated entirely to exploring how gospel-based nonviolence can contribute to the life and witness of the Catholic Church.

In writing *Love in Action*, I've drawn on over fifty years of involvement in direct-action organizing. It is my hope and prayer that this handbook will help concerned Catholics work more effectively for the reform and renewal of our beloved Church.

Richard K. Taylor

# Introduction

Many dedicated, creative reform and renewal groups have grown out of U. S. Catholicism.[1] Some have been working to achieve their goals for over forty years. These reform movements have held conferences, published newsletters, worked with the press, reached out to Church leaders, and engaged in a myriad of other reform activities. It seems safe to say, however, that none can claim to have achieved their main goals. Church reformers appear to be up against a brick wall.

It is not yet in the interest of leaders in the Catholic Church to take us seriously, much less to act on our proposals. For the most part, Church leaders rebuff or ignore us. Some groups have been denounced, banned from meeting on Church property, or even excommunicated (as was a Nebraska Call to Action group in 2006). Even if we don't face such drastic measures, we often feel treated like children who are to be seen and not heard, rather than thoughtful adults, with talents, intelligence, and experience that the Church desperately needs.

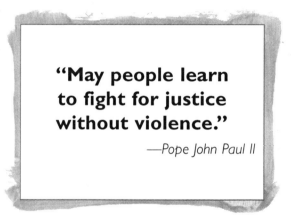

**"May people learn to fight for justice without violence."**

*—Pope John Paul II*

Tom Roberts, editor of the *National Catholic Reporter,* once characterized the contemporary situation as one in which the bishops are sinking in a mire of quicksand and the laity are standing on firm ground around the edge with ropes, offering to help. The bishops remonstrate, saying, "No, no, we can handle this ourselves."

Such treatment is hard on those working for reform. Discouragement sets in. Interest flags when it's hard to see meaningful change. When there's such a sense of impasse, group leaders burn out, and members begin to drop out.

This sense of stalemate has led some of us in the reform movement to speculate about whether nonviolent direct action, in the spirit of great pioneers like Mahatma Gandhi, Martin Luther King Jr., Dorothy Day, and Daniel Berrigan might help penetrate the brick wall. We see that nonviolent direct action has been a powerful force for social change, not only in well-known cases like India's liberation and the U.S. civil rights movement, but in many other places and times. Some of us have experienced the power of nonviolence directly by participating in direct-action campaigns. Could this power be harnessed to get past the wall of resistance we face from church leaders today?

Catholic reform groups have used a multitude of methods in pursuit of their goals. Some have even used means associated with nonviolent direct action, such as prayer vigils, rallies, marches, and picketing. Certainly all these methods are "nonviolent" in the sense that they do not engage in violence. But the great pioneers of nonviolence saw it as something both deeper and more profound than the levels to which most Catholic reform groups have taken it. Here is a definition of nonviolence that reflects that depth:

*Nonviolence is a faith-based method of working for human liberation. It uses careful strategies and long-term, momentum-building campaigns to oppose what is wrong, unfair, oppressive or unjust. At the same time, it reaches out to the perpetrators of the injustice, not with violence, but with a persistent, creative goodwill and realistic love. In expressing that love, it is willing to accept suffering rather than inflicting it on others.*

Pope John Paul II

Nonviolence in this sense aims at building not just occasional, discrete nonviolent *actions* but a nonviolent *movement* made up of direct-action *campaigns*—highly energized, intensely focused, concentrated streams of action with specific goals, steps, well-reasoned strategies, concrete time lines, and the expectation of success.

Nonviolence in its many forms has been used by millions of people around the world in many cultures and historical eras. (Theologian and social scientist Walter Wink estimates that when all nonviolent movements in all countries are included, more than *three billion* people were involved in active nonviolence in the twentieth century alone.) Nonviolent campaigns have overthrown repressive dictators, overcome colonialism, played a key role in dismantling Communism, thwarted invasions, helped women secure the right to vote, strengthened labor demands, supported human rights, helped farm workers, changed government policies, provided potent strategies for the environmental movement, and, in several countries during World War II, stopped Nazis from sending Jews to concentration camps.

The twenty-first century already has seen several powerful nonviolent movements. As recently as 2004–2005, tens of thousands of Ukrainians used nonviolent mass street demonstrations in their "orange revolution" movement to reverse a fraudulent election, bring down a corrupt ruler, and install Viktor Yushchenko as the country's new democratically elected president.[2]

Dr. Gene Sharp points out that since 1970, politically significant nonviolent action has taken place in Algeria, Argentina, Armenia, Australia, Bolivia, Bosnia, Brazil, Burma/Myanmar, Chile, China, Costa Rica, (former) East and West Germany, El Salvador, Estonia, France, Georgia, Haiti, India, Iran, Ireland, Japan, Latvia, Lithuania, Madagascar, Mexico, Moldova, Morocco, New Caledonia, Nicaragua, Nigeria, Norway, Pakistan, Panama, Philippines, Poland, South Africa, South Korea, Sudan, Thailand, the United States, and (former) Yugoslavia. Sharp notes, "Clearly some of the recent and current cases have not yet succeeded while others have produced dramatic changes, even toppling powerful established governments."[3]

In recent years, some Church leaders have come to recognize the power of nonviolence. The late Pope John Paul II's now-well-recognized involvement in the nonviolent movement to overthrow Communism in Eastern Europe, for example, gave him an unusual perspective on the active, dynamic nature of nonviolence. His appreciation for its power comes through especially in his encyclical *Centesimus Annus:*

> It seemed that the European order resulting from the Second World War . . . could only be overturned by another war. Instead, it has been overcome by the nonviolent commitment of people who, while always refusing to yield to the force of power, succeeded time after time in finding effective ways of bearing witness to the truth . . . May people learn to fight for justice without violence.[4]

Our own U.S. bishops, in their famous peace pastoral, described nonviolence as rooted in Scripture, the life of Christ, and the Church's tradition:

> The vision of Christian nonviolence is not passive about injustice and the defense of the rights of others . . . Nonviolence is not the way of the weak, the cowardly or the impatient . . . Spiritual writers have helped trace the theory of nonviolence to its roots in scripture and tradition and have illustrated its practice and success in their studies of the Church fathers and the age of martyrs. Christ's own teachings and example provide a model way of life incorporating the truth and a refusal to return evil for evil.[5]

**Catholic reform and renewal groups are not trying to replace the Church's leadership structure.**

In spite of its proven power and its compatibility with Christian faith, active nonviolence is not, for many Catholics, their "cup of tea." Even if they are very committed to Church renewal, they cannot see themselves participating in direct action in any form. They may feel it's fine to use direct action in other contexts, but not in efforts to reform the Church.[6] In many situations where reformers are working for change, it may be that nonviolent direct action will not be needed or appropriate. Certainly, direct action is not a cure-all. Many paths to renewal undoubtedly are needed. Who can say for sure what means are most relevant at a particular time in history to bring about needed changes?

However, given the historically attested power of active nonviolence, its roots in our Christian faith, and the fact that only a few of its methods have been drawn upon by reform groups, it certainly is worth considering as a promising approach to reform. With God's help, active nonviolence might bring to reality a Church more like the one of Jesus' dream.

This handbook assumes it *is* worth a try, and describes how to develop nonviolent, direct-action campaigns. Therefore, it is intended for those Catholics who sense that reform groups must find much more compelling methods than we have used so far to accomplish our mission and realize our goals. It is written for those who are willing to take a look at the potential of gospel nonviolence and, if so moved, to use it in their reform efforts.

Well-organized nonviolent direct action is a powerful means of working for social change. However, it is not a panacea. It doesn't always achieve its objectives. The forces of domination are strong and may sometimes win out. The end result may be a mix of success and failure. A successful nonviolent campaign requires much difficult organizing, patience, skill, humor, prayer, good timing, and creativity. At times, "success" may need to be redefined simply to mean "witnessing to the truth" or "doing our best to act as Jesus would," whether the outcome is victory or defeat. There is always another day to try again.

**Rosary**                     Julie Lonemann

It should be obvious, but perhaps it should be said, that Catholic reform and renewal groups, at least as understood here, are not trying to replace the Church's leadership structure. We respect the essential role of pope, bishops, and clergy in the Church. We accept the validity of authoritative leadership at the level of the universal Church, charged with safeguarding the Church's unity and preserving sound teaching.[7] We affirm the fundamental doctrines of the Church and have no desire to change them. We do not believe that the Church's problems today are caused by evil clerics clinging to power and trying to oppress the laity.[8]

In essence, we simply want the sacred dignity of every member of the Church to be respected and affirmed.

We want to open space within the Catholic Church so that we—in communion with the ordained and vowed religious—can exercise our full responsibility and express the fullness of our gifts for building up the Church (Eph. 2:19–22; 4:11–16) and for fulfilling the Christ-given task of going and making disciples of all nations (Matt. 28:19).

This is a task not just for the sake of the Church but for the sake of the world. A Church reformed and renewed can do *much* more to change the world. A reformed Church can work to diminish or transform hatred, injustice, oppression, racism, poverty, war, ecological destruction, killing of the innocent, and all the other evils that plague humanity. Ultimately, such a renewed faith community will lead the way in replacing these with freedom, love, and respect for life. "Your kingdom come, your will be done, *on earth* as it is in heaven."

# NOTES

1.  Some of the better-known groups are the Association for Rights of Catholics in the Church, Call to Action, Catholic Organizations for Renewal, Catholics Speak Out, CORPUS, Dignity USA, FutureChurch, National Federation of Priests' Councils, Priests for Equality, Voice of the Faithful, and the Women's Ordination Conference. (Of course, there are also more conservative or "restorationist" groups who see "reform" as going back to many aspects of the pre-Vatican II Church.)

2.  For descriptions of many successful nonviolent campaigns, see Peter Ackerman and Jack DuVall, *A Force More Powerful: A Century of Nonviolent Conflict* (New York: St. Martin's Press, 2000); Ronald Sider and Richard Taylor, *Nuclear Holocaust and Christian Hope* (Downers Grove: InterVarsity Press, 1982), Chapter 13; Robert Cooney and Helen Michalowski, *The Power of the People* (Culver City, CA: Peace Press, 1977); Louis Fischer, *The Life of Mahatma Gandhi* (New York: Harper, 1950); Martin Luther King Jr., *Stride Toward Freedom* (New York: Harper, 1958); Gene Sharp, *The Politics of Nonviolent Action* (Boston: Porter Sargent, 1973) and *Waging Nonviolent Struggle: 20$^{th}$ Century Practice and 21$^{st}$ Century Potential* (Boston: Porter Sargent, 2005).

3.  Gene Sharp, "Beyond Just War and Pacifism: Nonviolent Struggle Toward Justice, Freedom and Peace," *The Ecumenical Review*, Vol. 48, No. 2, April 1996, 237–8. In Chapter 2, we will describe in detail the deeply Catholic movement that overthrew Marcos.

4.  Encyclical Letter of John Paul II, *Centesimus Annus*: "On the Hundredth Anniversary of Rerum Novarum" (Rome: May 1, 1991, published in the U.S.A. by St. Paul Books and Media), 33–35.

5.  U.S. Bishops' Pastoral Letter on War and Peace, *The Challenge of Peace: God's Promise and Our Response* (Published in *Origens*, May 19, 1983), 9, 12, and 21.

6.  See the next chapter for a reflection on the appropriateness of using nonviolent direct action in efforts at Church reform.

7.  For more on "authoritative leadership" to preserve sound teaching, see Matt. 16:16–20; Vatican II, "Decree on Ecumenism," #2; "Dogmatic Constitution on the Church," #10, 18–25.

8.  Oppression, of course, can happen without the conscious intention to oppress. "The accusation of systemic or structural oppression of the laity ... does not ... require the claim that clergy consciously oppress or abuse nonclergy. Indeed, ... there are good reasons to see the oppressors ... as themselves oppressed. The claim is only that the division between clergy and laity ... systematically subordinates and undervalues the lay lifestyle, lay talent, lay leadership, lay experience and lay spirituality ... In fact the laity are systematically treated *as if* they have lesser talents and are of lesser account." Paul Lakeland, *The Liberation of the Laity* (New York: Continuum, 2003), 195.

# Chapter 1

# Nonviolent Direct Action for Church Reform?

The word *reform* is a positive term in Catholic teaching. In its "Decree on Ecumenism," the Church's Second Vatican Council (1962–65) teaches that the Church itself needs continual reform and renewal. It urges the Catholic faithful and all Christians to "undertake with vigor the task of renewal and reform" (#4). Christ himself, it says, summons the Church to "continual reformation" (#6).

Such teachings make clear that, while the Church is of divine origin, it walks with human feet. Christians, including Church leaders, make mistakes. Throughout its history, the Catholic Church has sparked reform and renewal movements aimed at correcting such mistakes while retaining the essentials of faith.

## REFORM IN THE MODERN CHURCH?

The epochal mistakes in the recent crisis surrounding clerical sex abuse are a modern case in point. Reform groups ask: Is this crisis a symptom of a much deeper malady than just the behavior of mentally and morally ill priests? Why have no bishops confessed that their infamous cover-up of the abuse was just as immoral as the perverse acts of individual priests? Why are they not held responsible for their own scandalous behavior? What role does clericalism play? What further reforms are needed to protect our children, to restore the Church's moral credibility, and to make sure the wretched behavior of sex abuse and cover-up stops?

Modern reform groups also are addressing the Church's failure to fully honor the dignity, wisdom, and gifts of women. Why are highly qualified women cut out of top-level ecclesiastical bodies? Why does the Vatican make gender a criterion for ordination? Why do Church leaders insist on sexist male language in liturgical and catechetical texts?

Other profound questions abound, fueling further efforts at reform and renewal. Many center on issues of finances and lifestyle. Why is there so much secrecy and so little financial transparency and accountability to the laity who support the Church financially? Why do serious financial scandals occur repeatedly? Why do so many Church leaders maintain princely lifestyles, so unlike that of Jesus? Why are our bishops found more often in the company of the rich and the powerful rather than with the poor and the oppressed? Where is their real passion for social justice and peace?

Furthermore, reform groups ask, why doesn't the Magisterium credit the *sensus fidelium* [sense of the faithful] on issues like contraception, sexuality, and family life? Why is the hierarchy so unwilling to restore the ancient practice of optional celibacy for clergy? Why are the talents, experience, and intelligence of the laity so often disdained and squandered? Why are qualified laity kept out of meaningful decision-making roles in Church governance? Why don't the laity have a role in selecting their priests and bishops, as was the case in the early Church? Why do Church leaders maintain a governing structure that some have called "the last feudal system in the West"?[1] Why haven't the bishops rallied Catholics across the world to protest unjust wars (such as in Iraq), as they have done with protests against abortion and same-sex marriage?

These are crucial questions. This handbook is written in the belief that concerned Catholics can use active nonviolence to address them and to spark meaningful reform.

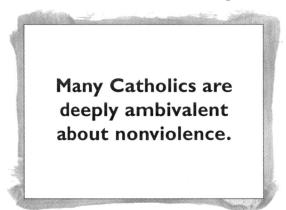

**Many Catholics are deeply ambivalent about nonviolence.**

However, it also recognizes that many Catholics, to the extent that we think about it at all, are deeply ambivalent about nonviolence. On the one hand, the courageous and powerful nonviolent witness of people like Martin Luther King, Jr., Cesar Chavez, Dorothy Day, and Mahatma Gandhi, incline many to respond favorably to the phrase "nonviolent direct action." It brings to mind positive images of people working powerfully but peacefully for important social changes. On the other hand, other Catholics find that the same words conjure up images of angry crowds and riots in the streets. Whatever our feelings about nonviolent direct action, we may question if it is an appropriate method to use in reforming the Church.

## NONVIOLENCE IN THE CHURCH FAMILY?

Many who experience the Church as family may be especially reticent to see the relevance of direct action for Church reform. "It's fine to march or sit in to achieve changes in society, such as overcoming racial segregation," they may say. "But is it right to use it within the Church family?"[2] They argue, "The Church is our mother. We may disagree strenuously with Mom at times, but is it right to march through her neighborhood, picket her house, or do sit-ins in her living room?"

The answer may seem obvious: Of course not. But measures that make sense when a family is functioning well may be inadequate when it is in trouble. We must consider what love may require in a well-functioning family as compared to a family in crisis.

When you love someone in your family, you want what is best for them. Love is more than a feeling. Love means extending and even sacrificing oneself for the sake of the loved one.[3] Such self-forgetting love springs up naturally in families, as when parents stay up with an inconsolable baby crying in the wee hours of the morning. Most of us know love first in our families. If we're fortunate, our families are our first Church—the place where we first learn about Jesus and his love. It is the place where we begin to practice love of God, neighbor, and self.

But sometimes a family can become dysfunctional. Family members might get into alcoholism, illegal drugs, spouse abuse, or other serious moral and legal crises. Love calls us to reach out to such persons. We reason with them, plead with them, urge them to get help.

But these family members may resist, be defensive, or rationalize. They may disdain our advice or turn their backs on us. Rather than throw up our hands, we may do something more drastic. We may organize an "intervention" in which a group of family and friends insist on meeting with the person to explain the destructive impact of his or her behavior. We demand that the one we love get help. We refuse to take no for an answer. At times, we may have to restrain them for their own good—or even commit them to a helping program or call the police. Such times call for tough love, not sentimental love.

When we get frustrated and angry with those we love, our love requires us to persevere, to go out of ourselves for the sake of the beloved. We know their potential. We remember what they were like in better days. We are drawn by our belief in what they could be.

> **We see the Church's potential. We are drawn by a vision of what it could be.**

## DYSFUNCTIONAL FAMILY, DYSFUNCTIONAL CHURCH

We also love the family that is the Catholic Church. We are active Catholics and we celebrate the many, many good things about the Church, in its present and in its past.

But the Church, too, can become a dysfunctional family. Some of its members or leaders can do terrible things, as the clergy sex-abuse crisis has revealed. What could be more dysfunctional than trusted priests sexually abusing the innocent children placed in their care? What could be more dysfunctional than bishops transferring abusing priests from one assignment to another, even with letters of recommendation, in apparent indifference to the suffering of preyed-upon children?[4]

We are outraged and feel betrayed. Even more, we feel a great sadness over what has happened. We know that these crimes, these cover-ups, and this destruction of innocent lives are not the true nature of the Church. This is not what Christ wants. We remember what our Church was like in better days. We see its potential. We are drawn by a vision of what it could be.

At such times, isn't it valid to do an intervention in this family we call "the Church"? Isn't it warranted to bring pressure to bear and to insist on change? Isn't it legitimate to try not just ordinary love but the tough love of nonviolent direct action?

# NOTES

1. Fr. Donald Cozzens, *Faith That Dares to Speak* (Collegeville: Liturgical Press, 2004), 12.

2. Pope Leo XIII called the family "the first form of the Church on earth" (*Arcanum Divine Sapientiae,* "On Christian Marriage," 1880). Vatican Council II (1962–65) declared that the family is "the domestic Church" ("Dogmatic Constitution on the Church," n. 11). Pope John Paul II said, "The family. . . . can and should be called 'the domestic Church'" ("Apostolic Exhortation on the Family," n. 21, 1981).

3. St. Paul defined love in this same way when he asked the Corinthian Church to participate generously in the collection for Jerusalem. He saw members' willingness to give relief generously as a way "to test the genuineness of your love by your concern for others" (2 Cor. 8:8).

4. Regarding the responsibility of Church leaders in clerical sex abuse, business executive Frederick W. Gluck asks this pointed question: "What would we think if the retail banking division of a financial conglomerate discovered that 5 percent of its tellers were embezzling money, and simply moved them from branch to branch . . . without . . . exposing the offenders to the justice system or even informing the employees' new supervisors of their history?" ("The Pope as Chief Executive," *The Financial Times*, May 7, 2005).

# Chapter 2

# Gospel Nonviolence

*What we call nonviolence is simply living out the Gospel. It includes a commitment to respect the sacredness of each person and the determination to overcome all domination.*

— *Archbishop Dom Helder Camara, Brazil*

Hundreds of thousands of Christians have practiced gospel nonviolence throughout history. They have done so as individuals, as Church members, in groups, and in movements. Rooted in Christ-centered faith, they have resisted what they saw as wrong, while reaching out to the wrongdoers—not with violence, but with goodwill and persistent love. They were willing to take suffering on themselves rather than inflict it on others. In this way they modeled the nonviolence of the gospels.

This handbook assumes contemporary Church reform groups can do the same. In order to examine more deeply the meaning of gospel nonviolence, this chapter offers three case studies of gospel nonviolence, then looks at the nonviolence of Jesus and the nonviolence of the early Christian Church.

**Catherine of Siena**   by Br. R. Lentz, OFM
© 1995 Image courtesy of www.TrinityStores.com
800.699.4482

## ST. CATHERINE OF SIENA: CHAMPION OF CHURCH REFORM

In fourteenth century Avignon, where Pope Clement V had relocated the papacy from Rome, a succession of popes lived luxuriously in a great palace overlooking the Rhone River. Here, cardinals vied with one another for the most opulent suites. "One required ten stables for his horses, and another rented parts of fifty-one houses to lodge all his retainers."[1]

Catherine of Siena (later made a saint and doctor of the Church) arrived in the city in 1376, convinced Christ had called her there to confront the pope. Like her contemporary, Bridget of Sweden, she denounced the corruption of the hierarchy and called for massive Church reform.

Before arriving in Avignon, she traveled, spoke to growing crowds, met with Church leaders and government officials, and wrote to the pope with audacious language: "Be a man, Father. Arise! No negligence! Do God's will and mine . . . I am telling you."[2] Finally, she had an audience with Pope Gregory XI and laid out what can only be described as "demands" for Church reform. Though she was called "a wretched little woman" by three theologians appointed to examine her orthodoxy and was in danger of being brought before the Inquisition, Catherine touched Gregory so deeply that he acceded. In fear and trembling, he returned to Rome. The "Babylonian Exile" of the Church was over, and fires of reform were reignited.

Entrance to Auschwitz-Birkenau concentration camp

Catherine's dramatic actions—resisting Church corruption, confronting those who could cause her great suffering, yet always reaching out to power-holders with the transforming belief that they could change—illustrate how nonviolent actions by a deeply centered individual can bring about prodigious renewal.

## EUROPEAN CHRISTIANS RESIST THE NAZI "FINAL SOLUTION"

Fast forward more than five centuries. The Nazi occupiers of France were determined to round up Jews and send them to the death camps. André Trocmé, a Protestant pastor and pacifist, turned the village and region of Le Chambon into a network of people who hid Jews and sent them to safety in Switzerland. When a Vichy official came to inspect Trocmé's school, thirty students handed him a letter stating: "We have learned that in Paris, Jews are herded into the stadium and then deported. After that, all trace of them is lost. This, in our Christian eyes, is unbearable . . . We will not obey [such an order] if applied here . . . No matter what the government orders, we will hide Jews."[3]

Later on, after townspeople had helped many Jews escape into Switzerland, the Gestapo threatened to level the town in retaliation. But the local German commandant, impressed by the consistently firm but loving demeanor of the resisters, refused to allow it. By these and similar actions elsewhere, about 75 percent of French Jews escaped Nazi grasp.[4]

Hundreds of miles to the east, Metropolitan Stefan of the Bulgarian Orthodox Church not only spoke out against persecution of the Jews, but

*LOVE IN ACTION*

hid the chief Rabbi of Sofia in his home. Orthodox Bishop Kiril told King Boris that if deportations were ordered, he would lead a campaign of civil disobedience against them, "including personally lying down on the railroad tracks before the deportation trains."[5] Due to such nonviolent resistance by Christian leaders and many ordinary Bulgarians, none of the country's fifty thousand Jews were deported or killed.

Similar nonviolent action campaigns saved thousands of Jews in countries like Denmark, Norway, Finland, Holland, and Italy. Thousands of resisters paid a heavy price for their courage: torture, death by hanging in public squares, and death by gassing in concentration camps. Their heroic actions stand in vivid contrast to the timidity of the Catholic Church[6] at large and the failure of the vast majority of European non-Jews to speak or act against the Nazi genocide. What might have happened if the *majority* of European Christians had chosen the way of Jesus and the path of nonviolent resistance?

## FILIPINO CHRISTIANS BRING DOWN A DICTATOR

The modern era has seen a swell of powerful nonviolent movements. One example that deserves a detailed description is the 1980s struggle in the Philippines against the dictatorship of Ferdinand Marcos. This struggle was particularly significant because of the deep and crucial involvement of Catholics and the extensive organizing done to maintain non-violence and make the effort successful.[7]

It's All Over
photo by pa.eng, http://peoplepower.e-workers.de

Marcos began as a reformer, but his twenty-year reign accumulated increasing levels of corruption and cronyism. Under his rule reformers were jailed and tortured. One of them, the highly popular Benigno Aquino, was assassinated. Aquino's devout Catholic wife, Corazon Aquino, visited a convent and asked a priest to offer masses in his memory, stressing the nonviolent response her husband would have wanted from the people.

As a result, Jean and Hildegard Goss-Myer, European Catholics and internationally-known nonviolence trainers, were invited to travel around the country and share their extensive experience in direct action. Over more than a year, they offered dozens of seminars and trainings in faith-based nonviolence to union leaders, opposition politicians, base Christian communities, bishops, priests, nuns, and seminarians. They emphasized not only the methods of nonviolence, but also Jesus' message of the liberating power of truth and love.

In the process, they helped organize more than sixty groups committed to nonviolent change. The movement came to be known as *AKKAP-KA,* a Tagalog word meaning "nonviolent action." They also used the name *Alaydaland* (which means "offer dignity") to express their understanding of nonviolence.

In 1986, Marcos called for presidential elections. Immediately, Cory Aquino announced her opposition candidacy. To try to keep the election clean and fair, AKKAPKA recruited and trained five hundred thousand volunteers to serve both as election monitors and as nonviolent resisters should the elections prove fraudulent. They developed scenarios for possible election outcomes and plans for how to respond nonviolently to each eventuality. They distributed widely the writings of Gandhi and Martin Luther King Jr. and set up tent cities with "prayer tents." Training in nonviolence took place every morning; the Eucharist was celebrated every day at noon.

On election day, February 7, when it was clear that massive fraud was being committed, tens of thousands of people wrapped themselves around ballot boxes, singing religious songs and praying the rosary. When Marcos supporters announced that he had been reelected, crowds of angry demonstrators formed in protest. Priests and nuns entered the crowds, exhorting them to nonviolence and explaining its methods. (NBC News in the United States noted that they were "trained by experts in nonviolence.")

On Sunday, February 9, Manila's Cardinal Jaime Sin led a Mass for Cory Aquino before ten thousand enthusiastic worshipers, expressing gratitude for "a true awakening among our people." Soon after, the hierarchy issued a strong statement, calling the Marcos election fraudulent.

When two top military men publicly agreed with the Cardinal and called on soldiers to rebel, military defectors left their units and holed up in camps only four miles from the presidential palace. With troops still loyal to Marcos threatening to attack, tens of thousands of civilians used their bodies to form a human screen around the camps. "We will die here if we have to," said Faustino Olaguera, a businessman. "We will die standing up. We have no arms." When troops loyal to Marcos shot at the defecting soldiers, resisters threw themselves in front of the soldiers to protect them.

At one point, Marcos ordered his air force to attack one of the camps, only to have the entire unit disobey. This prompted Marcos to send one thousand troops, with tanks and armored personnel carriers, against the rebels. Their advance was blocked by twenty-five thousand civilians, including many priests and nuns. They spoke in a friendly way to the helmeted heads protruding from the tanks. They explained their movement and urged the soldiers not to fire on their brothers and sisters, who were only fighting for their freedom. The troops stopped in their tracks; no shots were fired.

The crowd of nonviolent defenders eventually grew to several hundred thousand. At one point, Cory Aquino spoke to a crowd estimated at one million. Marcos' former chief of staff went on the radio to say, "It is now more honorable to be killed by this regime than to fight and die for it."

Ferdinand Marcos vowed "to fight to the last ounce of blood," but his calls to his troops and civilian supporters fell on deaf ears. In the face of such massive nonviolent resistance, it became impossible for Marcos to hold onto power. Two weeks after election day, he resigned and left the country.

Jubilant crowds surged through the streets, carrying statues of the Virgin Mary and crowns of thorns they had fashioned out of barbed wire. At her first press conference as president, Cory Aquino said:

> The world saw and recorded a people who knelt in the path of oncoming tanks and subdued with embraces of

Photo by Corazon Pasiona from *People Power: An Eyewitness History,*
published by the James B. Reuter, SJ foundation.

friendship the battle-hardened troops sent out to disperse them and annihilate the military rebels. All the world wondered as they witnessed, in the space of two months, a people lift themselves from humiliation to the greatest pride. I am fortunate to be the president of a people who have demonstrated such courage.

## JESUS AND THE FOUNDATIONS OF GOSPEL NONVIOLENCE

In each of the cases above, five common themes emerge: (1) deep faith, (2) resistance to injustice, (3) goodwill toward wrongdoers, (4) willingness to suffer for what is right, and (5) refusal to inflict suffering on others. These themes are embodied in the life of Jesus, whose example, guidance, and inspiration permeated not only these struggles, but thousands of others from Christ's resurrection until now.

Gandhi

What distinguishes gospel nonviolence is its firm grounding in Jesus Christ's life, teachings, example, death, resurrection, and ongoing guidance. This is not to disparage other forms of nonviolence that arise from other traditions. After all, Gandhi, a Hindu, was a pioneer in creative, active nonviolent resistance.

Interestingly, Gandhi acknowledged Jesus' strong influence on his nonviolent philosophy. "The Sermon on the Mount went straight to my heart," he wrote.[8] A biographer noted that the only picture on the walls of Gandhi's mud hut was a picture of Jesus.[9] Perhaps if we Christians reflected on Jesus' life and teachings as deeply as did Gandhi, many more of us would be committed to nonviolent social change.

In Jesus, we have a unique and powerful embodiment of nonviolence. As Christians, we can walk consciously in prayer with the resurrected Christ today, receiving his love, forgiveness, strength, and guidance as we seek loving ways to overcome injustice and oppression.

Pope John Paul II put this companionship movingly when he said:

Jesus . . . proposes a communion of life which is not sporadic but continuous and genuine. He does not ask us to find it outside us or near us, but within, where he dwells, in the depths of our hearts. How essential it is to practice listening to his voice which speaks in silence!

And then we need to devote time to getting to know this Friend, to learning how to think like him, to evaluate, as he does, the events in our personal and social life and, like him, to make a generous and consistent response (Rome, 7/19/91).

Much has been written on Jesus as a model of nonviolence. Perhaps new light can be shed by reflecting briefly on how Jesus embodies the five foundational themes of nonviolence.

# FAITH

It almost goes without saying that Jesus' faith in and obedience to God was absolute. In spite of being tempted, he was so deeply centered and at one with God that he never turned away from that path. He declared at the outset of his ministry, "One does not live by bread alone, but by every word that comes from the mouth of God" (Matt. 4:4). "The Son can do nothing on his own," he said after a healing, "but only what he sees the Father doing; for whatever the Father does, the Son does likewise" (John 5:19). "My Father, if it is possible," he said at the close of his life, "let this cup pass from me; yet, not as I will, but as you will" (Matt. 26:39).

Jesus recognized the human limitations that so often make us those "of little faith" (Luke 12:28). Still, he encouraged his disciples—and encouraged us, his followers today—to "have faith in God" (Mark 11:22). He promised that we too will do great things, even if our faith is as small as a mustard seed (Matt. 17:20). Deep faith character-ized Jesus. Such faith has characterized every move-ment of gospel nonviolence since his time.

## RESISTANCE TO INJUSTICE

Jesus was outspoken in his challenges to the wrongs he saw being committed by some religious and political leaders of his day. He excoriated those scribes and Pharisees who treated vulnerable widows unjustly, who valued external appearances over inter-nal integrity, who showed a gap between their pro-fessed faith and their actual practices (see Matt. 23:2–33, Mark 12:38–40). When a woman alleged to have been caught in adultery was brought before him, he courageously and nonviolently prevented a group of self-righteous men from stoning her to death (John 8:1–11). As Fr. John Dear, SJ, said in his little book, *Disarming the Heart,* "Jesus' way of love did not mean passivity or apathy but meant standing up for what was right. It meant non-cooperation with evil and violence and overcoming that evil and violence through love and truth and a willingness to suffer for love and truth."[10]

Julie Lonemann

Jesus' resistance to injustice, oppression, and wrong was based on his affirmation of the infinite value of every human life. "Suppose one of you has only one sheep," he queried some Pharisees, "and it falls into a pit on the Sabbath; will you not lay hold of it and lift it out? How much more valu-able is a human being than a sheep!" (Matt. 12:11–12). Much of Jesus' day-to-day ministry involved lifting people out of pits. He liberated captives, whatever their form of captivity. His heart went out to humans flounder-ing in sinkholes of sickness, blindness, guilt, demon-possession, ignorance, or confusion. He moved quickly to respond to their needs. He did so even if it meant breaking a law or putting his own life at risk (see Matt. 12:2; Mark 2:23–24; 3:1–6; Luke 14:1–6; John 5:1–16).

For Jesus, human laws, customs, and institutions are meant for human liberation, not the other way around (Mark 2:27). Jesus' lawbreaking stands in a long line of courageous Jewish men and women who committed civil disobedience by violating laws, customs, or edicts that did not follow the way of love and truth.[11] It continued in the early Church and continues today as people disobey unjust laws and risk imprisonment for the sake of justice and peace.

## GOODWILL TOWARD WRONGDOERS

For Jesus, love of God and neighbor were the two basic commandments (Matt. 22:37–40; Mark 12:29–31; Luke 10:27–28). When asked "Who is my neighbor?" he told the Good Samaritan story to show that "neighbor" means anyone in need and "love" means taking concrete action to meet their need (Luke 10:25–37). Jesus called his followers to love even their enemies:

**The Good Samaritan**          *M. P. Wiggins*

But I say to you that listen, love your enemies, do good to those who hate you, bless those who curse you, pray for those who abuse you. If anyone strikes you on one cheek, offer the other also . . . If you love those who love you, what credit is that to you? Even sinners love those who love them . . . But love your enemies, do good and lend, expecting nothing in return. Your reward will be great, and you will be children of the Most High; for he is kind to the ungrateful and the wicked. Be merciful, just as your Father is merciful (Luke 6:27–36).

Jesus, of course, not only preached love of enemies; he lived it. He expressed this love throughout his life, always seeking to engage his enemies, never trying to hurt them. He manifested this at the very end on the cross, when he incarnated his own command to "bless those who curse you, pray for those who mistreat you" (Luke 6:28) by asking, "Father, forgive them, for they know not what they do" (Luke 23:34).

There have been thousands of movements against perceived injustices throughout history. Few have tried to restrain the hatred that is almost inevitable in such contests. What is most striking about nonviolent movements is their determination, like that of Jesus, not to hate but to love.

# WILLINGNESS TO SUFFER

The God of Jesus Christ, says theologian Gil Bailie, "is a God who chooses to suffer violence rather than to sponsor it."[12] During his ministry Jesus upset his disciples by speaking of the cross and even asking them to take up their own cross, and follow him (Luke 9:13). He made clear that following him would lead to suffering, but he promised great blessing to those who were reviled and persecuted for his sake (Matt. 5:11–12).

As his young life drew to a close, Jesus knew his decision to go to Jerusalem would put his life at risk. His friends warned him that the trip was too dangerous. But for the sake of the truth and love for which he stood and which he embodied, he traveled to exactly where his enemies were determined to kill him. Loving his enemies, he reached out constantly with passionate, self-giving *agape* to all.

When he was arrested, he accepted blows and vilification without fighting back. When finally he was nailed in agony to the cross, he forgave those who abused and killed him. As John Dear comments, "Hanging naked on the cross, Jesus was completely disarmed and responded only with love, forgiveness, and truth."[13] From the perspective of nonviolence, Jesus' self-sacrificial death on the cross was the ultimate act of nonviolence.

Again, it was Mohandas Gandhi, the Hindu, who articulated this as well as any Christian: "If you want something really important to be done, you must not merely satisfy the reason, you must move the heart also. The appeal of reason is more to the head, but the penetration of the heart comes from suffering."[14]

**Tree of Life**

*Julie Lonemann*

# REFUSAL TO INFLICT SUFFERING ON OTHERS

The history of Israel is full of armed and unarmed struggle—battles to enter the promised land, combat with surrounding peoples, resistance to foreign invaders, and liberation struggles against conquerors. Israelites were proud of their military victories. The Maccabees' defeat of powerful Syrian armies in 164 BC is still celebrated by Jews in the festival of Hanukkah. Roman armies, however, were too powerful; the Palestine into which Jesus was born had been under Roman military occupation for more than sixty years.

The conflict between brutal Roman rule and Jewish aspirations for freedom frequently provoked Jewish armed rebellion. Just after Jesus' birth, such a rebellion was put down by the Roman governor of Syria, who crucified two thousand Jews in Jerusalem. The Jewish underground movement known as the Zealots believed slaying the godless was a religious duty and that a popular revolution against Rome would usher in a new age.

It was in occupied territory and in this highly charged atmosphere, then, that Jesus told his disciples to love their enemies—including despised Roman oppressors—and to turn the other cheek and go the second mile. Never did he inflict violence or suffering on his enemies, not even in his cleansing of the temple (Matt. 21:12; Mark 11:15; John 2:14-16).[15] Over and over, his life expressed unconditional love for all people, based on the very nature of God, who "makes his sun rise on the bad and the good" (Matt. 5:44–48).

> **Who could have predicted at the time that the followers of this gentle, crucified, apparently defeated Messiah would outlast the entire Roman Empire and win over its emperor?**

At the time of his arrest, Jesus told Peter that he could have called upon "more than twelve legions of angels" to protect him, but instead he ordered a follower who tried to defend him to put his sword back into its place, "for all who take the sword will perish by the sword" (Matt. 26:51–53).

In Jesus, then—in what he said and did and in how he died—we can find profound inspiration for our own commitment to overcome injustice and oppression through the way of nonviolence. Who could have predicted at the time that the followers of this gentle, crucified, apparently defeated Messiah would outlast the entire Roman Empire and win over its emperor?

## THE NONVIOLENT METHODS OF THE EARLY CHURCH

Still more inspiration can be found in the early Church, where those who were closest to Jesus historically replicated his nonviolent approach. The members of the early Church were not perfect people, any more than Jesus' first disciples. There were personality clashes, disagreements and other human foibles. Yet in their faithfulness to Jesus, they reproduced in remarkable ways and with uncommon consistency the nonviolence of Jesus.

Prior to Constantine's conversion, Roman emperors mounted ten major campaigns against the fledgling Church. Christians were imprisoned, tortured, executed, torn to pieces, and burned alive. They learned the meaning of Jesus' words, "Whoever would come after me must deny himself, take up his cross, and follow me" (Mark 8:34). Why weren't they crushed, as were so many movements before them?

Of course, much more than nonviolent resistance and love of enemies was involved here. Central to resisting the Empire and ultimately converting its emperor was Christian preaching of the gospel message, the power of the Holy Spirit, the love expressed in compassionate care for the poor, and the incorporation of new converts into a beloved community.

But it is just as clear that the gospel would not have been heard and accepted had it not been embodied in people who, within the limits of human frailty, were living it out. Jesus became real to the pagan world not only because pagans heard the gospel but also because they met disciples. They saw a company of people whose lives had been transformed by the Holy Spirit, who were trying to follow Jesus, and who, like their Lord, stood up against oppression with sacrificial love. The gospel of the cross became real because non-Christians saw Christians bearing their own crosses in a myriad of confrontations with evil. The early Church overcame Roman tyranny by the power of the gospel and the power of loving nonviolence.[16]

> **The gospel of the cross became real because non-Christians saw Christians bearing their own crosses in a myriad of confrontations with evil.**

Like nearly every instance of effective nonviolent action throughout history, the church demonstrated its strong resistance to injustice. Christians firmly opposed all Roman efforts to stamp out the Church. While some Christians broke under persecution and fled or renounced their faith, the Church's official stance was to refuse any step which required a Christian to violate his or her beliefs.

Christian leaders unleashed a torrent of protest, defiance, and censure against their persecutors and their decrees. Ordinary Christians tore down edicts of persecution, openly rebuked judges for ruthless sentences, and refused demands for sacrifice to heathen gods or to make an oath of fealty to the emperor. In the gladiatorial games, Christians condemned to undergo a boxing contest went on a hunger strike and refused the necessary training. "A Christian woman, dragged to the altar and commanded to sacrifice upon it, kicked it over."[17]

The early Christians refused to kill or to use violence. Their response to Roman oppression was active resistance characterized by a willingness to suffer and an active love toward their persecutors. St. Chrysostom, a fourth-century Christian leader, put it succinctly when he said: "What, then, ought we not to resist an evil? Indeed we ought; but not by retaliation. Christ hath commanded us to give up ourselves to suffering wrongfully, for thus we shall prevail over evil. For one fire is not quenched by another fire, but fire by water."[18]

The "water" they poured on the fire was not just a willingness to suffer but also loving their enemies and praying for them, as Jesus had taught. The Greek leader Aristeides said of the Christians, "They appeal to those who wrong them and make them friendly to themselves; they are eager to do good to their enemies."[19] The *Epistle to Diognetus,* written by Christian apologists in the first half of the second century, says that Christians "are reviled and they bless;" "they are insulted and are respectful."[20] A Christian, Justinus, said, "We pray for our enemies and try to persuade those who hate us unjustly."[21] The Church leader Tertullian told Church members that love of enemies is "the principle precept" of Christian life.[22] When St. Cyprian confronted his persecutors, he said, "It is not lawful for us to hate, and so we please God more when we render no requital for injury . . . We repay your hatred with kindness."

With such a "great cloud of witnesses" around us—Jesus, the early Church, and Christian disciples down through history—we too can find the courage and inspiration to set out on the path of gospel nonviolence. The rest of this book explores how to follow this path in our efforts to reform and renew the Church.

**The Spirit Hovers**

*Julie Lonemann*

*LOVE IN ACTION*

# NOTES

1. Robert McClory, *Faithful Dissenters: Stories of Men and Women Who Loved and Changed the Church* (New York: Orbis Books, 2001), 78. (See Barbara W. Tuchman, *A Distant Mirror: The Calamitous Fourteenth Century* (New York: Knopf, 1978), 28.)

2. McClory, 86.

3. Alan A. Hunter, *Christians in the Arena* (Nyack: Fellowship Publications, 1958), 40.

4. John Ferguson, *The Politics of Love* (Greenwood: Attic Press, n.d.), 108. The full story of the Le Chambon resistance is told in Philip Hallie, *Lest Innocent Blood Be Shed* (New York: Harper, 1979) and in the dramatic film by Pierre Sauvage, *Weapons of the Spirit* (1989).

5. Nora Levin, *The Holocaust* (New York: Schocken Books, 1973), 553, and Frederick B. Chary, *The Bulgarian Jews and the Final Solution 1940–44* (Pittsburgh: University of Pittsburgh Press, 1972), 90.

6. The role of the Catholic Church during the Holocaust has been debated endlessly. The Church's stance, while not as gutless as pictured by its worst detractors, certainly merits the term "timidity."

7. Accounts of the Philippine struggle were garnered from a variety of magazines, newspapers, and other reports.

8. Louis Fischer, *The Life of Mahatma Gandhi* (New York: Harper, 1950), 37. Fischer writes, "Next to Hinduism, he was most attracted by Christianity. He loved Jesus."; 333.

9. Herrymon Maurer, *Great Soul: the Growth of Gandhi* (Garden City: The Country Life Press, 1950), 82.

10. John Dear, *Disarming the Heart* (New York: Paulist Press, 1987), 109–110.

11. Here are a few examples of "civil disobedience" in the Hebrew Bible. The midwives Shiphrah and Puah refused to follow Pharaoh's order to kill newborn Jewish boys; they "were God-fearing and so did not obey the king" (Exod. 1:15–17). Moses' parents hid him, then put him in a basket by the Nile, disobeying Pharaoh's command to drown all boy babies by throwing them into the Nile (Exod. 2:1–4). Mordecai disobeyed King Ahasuerus's order to bow down to prime minister Haman, provoking the latter to plot the Jews' destruction because "they do not keep the king's laws" (Esther 3:2–9). Queen Esther went into the king's presence without being summoned, even though, for those who do so, "there is but one law—all alike are to be put to death" (Esther 4:1–5:7). Daniel was thrown into the lion's den when, by his faithful prayers, he violated "the law of the Medes and the Persians, which cannot be revoked" (Dan. 6:8–16). Shadrach, Meshach, and Abednego were thrown into the fiery furnace for refusing the king's order to worship the golden statue he had made (Dan. 3:1–30).

12. Gil Bailie, *Violence Unveiled* (New York: Crossroads, 1995), 66.

13. Dear, *Disarming the Heart*, 115.

14. Krishna Kripalani, ed., *Gandhi: All Men Are Brothers* (New York: Continuum, 1982), 82.

15. The much-debated cleansing of the temple often is interpreted as a justification for followers of Jesus to use violence. Clearly, however, the cleansing was an example, not of violence, but of Jesus' outrage expressed through overwhelming moral authority. He overturned the tables, but there is no evidence that he harmed the money changers. He used the whip on cattle, not people.

16. Much of this paragraph is taken from Ronald J. Sider and Richard K. Taylor, *Nuclear Holocaust and Christian Hope* (Downers Grove: InterVarsity Press, 1982), 255.

17. These observations on the early Church are drawn from Cecil John Cadoux, *The Early Church and the World* (Edinburgh: Clark, 1955), 531–555.

18. Quoted in C. G. H. Macgregor, *The New Testament Basis of Pacifism* (Nyack: Fellowship Publications, 1954), 154.

19. C. John Cadoux, *The Early Christian Attitude to War* (New York: Seabury Press, 1982), 73.

20. Ibid.

21. Cadoux, *The Early Church and the World*, 237.

22. Ronald Bainton, *Christian Attitudes Toward War and Peace* (Nashville: Abingdon, 1960), 77.

# Chapter 3

# The Twelve Steps of Gospel Nonviolence

Alcoholics Anonymous (AA) pioneered its well-known twelve-step program to help alcoholics in their recovery. Recovering alcoholics know they will never be free from the temptation to drink, but by attending AA meetings and "working the program," they can resist the enticement of drink and remain sober.

Nonviolent campaign-building has its own twelve-step program, designed to help its practitioners remain smart, strong, prayerful, and loving in their work for justice, even in the face of intransigence or hostility. Nonviolent campaigners know they will never be free of the temptation to let their anger overflow into combative animosity or violence of word or deed. However, by following the program, they can keep a nonviolent attitude, build strong direct-action groups, choose the best strategies, and take the other actions necessary for building an effective, nonviolent campaign.

**Early Christians**                    *M. P. Wiggins*

The nonviolent struggle against systems of domination can be very challenging. Often, people fail to join a direct-action campaign because it seems too daunting or because they think they don't know how to execute such a campaign. Maybe they feel they simply are too angry, impatient, or prone to violence. Perhaps they think nonviolent campaign-building requires the charisma of a Gandhi or a King. But nonviolence is not for super-people. It is a path for regular, wounded, cranky, sinful human beings. Most nonviolent movements throughout history have been carried out by just such ordinary people.[1]

The twelve steps below are meant to demystify what it takes to build a nonviolent campaign. The campaign may center around a single powerful action. Most campaigns, however, involve a number of direct actions, one building on another. The forms these direct actions take will vary tremendously, from prayer services and letter campaigns to civil disobedience. Chapter 4 is entirely devoted to the many creative and diverse forms nonviolent action may take.

Whatever actions you decide on, these twelve steps offer a clear, methodical framework that can be followed by any group willing to "work the program" and to practice love in action.

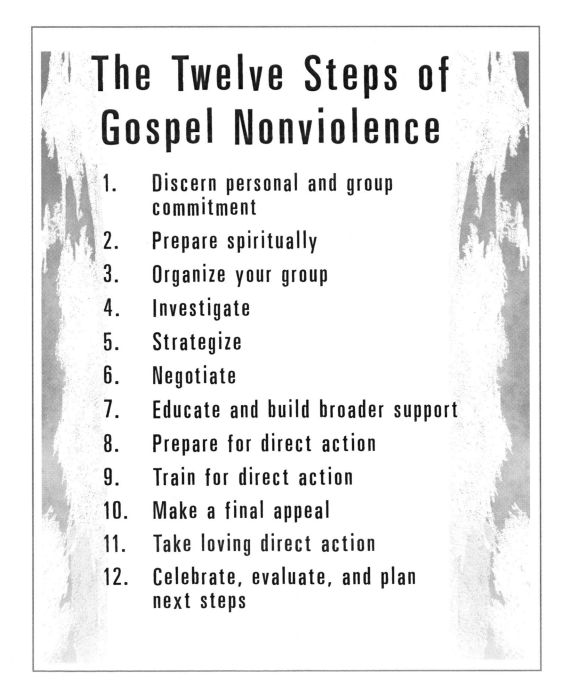

# The Twelve Steps of Gospel Nonviolence

1. Discern personal and group commitment

2. Prepare spiritually

3. Organize your group

4. Investigate

5. Strategize

6. Negotiate

7. Educate and build broader support

8. Prepare for direct action

9. Train for direct action

10. Make a final appeal

11. Take loving direct action

12. Celebrate, evaluate, and plan next steps

# BE CREATIVE WHILE FOLLOWING THE STEPS

The order of steps leading to any nonviolent direct-action is always somewhat arbitrary and does not always follow in sequence.[2] Like life itself, a nonviolent campaign is complex. The unexpected is to be expected. You cannot plan for every contingency. Any campaign as well as any single direct action requires art and creativity along with planning.

Therefore, there is nothing sacred about the twelve steps described below or the order in which they are given. It is a rare direct-action campaign that follows these steps in this exact order. For example, Steps 1 through 5 are continuous—they go on all the time. Your campaign, if well run, will educate and build broader support not only at Step 7, but throughout its entire course. Or, you may find that, after negotiating with power-holders (Step 6), you realize you don't have enough information and your group needs to go back and do more investigation (Step 4).

However, the steps do have a logical flow. One step builds on another. It doesn't make sense, for example, to leap into direct action without laying a groundwork of investigation, strategizing, and public education. Think carefully before you skip over a step or change the order. Your group should have a good reason to do so. Remember that the steps are drawn from the experience of nonviolent campaigners worldwide. But know you can shape them to your own needs.

**Banquet**                    *M. P. Wiggins*

## A PREFERENCE FOR SETTLEMENT

The steps below are *not* meant to be a "slippery slope," which inevitably lead to confrontations like picketing or sit-ins. Both Gandhi and King frequently expressed a strong preference for settlement through negotiation rather than having to use demonstrations to achieve their goals. If the issue can be settled at Step 6 or 7, there's no need to use demonstrations.

Bernard Lafayette was one of Martin Luther King's closest associates, a brilliant organizer who was jailed, tear-gassed, and beaten many times during the civil rights movement. Talking about the difficult problems that sometimes arise in nonviolent action, he said: "If you're motivated by love for people, you'll tend to come up with the right action."

Remember, you may not be an expert in nonviolent campaign-building, but you are the expert on your own local reality. The best nonviolent campaign-building will happen as you carefully study your own situation—and then apply to it what seems most relevant from this book and other sources. Ensuing chapters are written in outline format so you can use headings as guides and consult in-depth specifics as you need to.

# Step 1:
# Discern Personal and Group Commitment

**D**eveloping a campaign of active nonviolence can be exciting, fulfilling, even fun. Sometimes we join without deep discernment because we feel strongly about the issue it will address, because we trust the people planning the campaign, or because we feel right away that God is calling us to such involvement.

But a campaign can be very intense. It can involve risks, sacrifices, and large chunks of time. It is important, therefore, to think and pray carefully before committing yourself to a campaign. Here are four questions to ask yourself and the group with whom you're considering campaigning. (Also, it would be beneficial to explore these questions with family, friends, or other trusted people.)

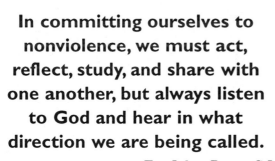

**In committing ourselves to nonviolence, we must act, reflect, study, and share with one another, but always listen to God and hear in what direction we are being called.**

—*Fr. John Dear, SJ*

1. Are we convinced that the situation or issue the campaign is addressing truly *is* unjust or wrong? Do we feel strongly about it? Do we want to make a personal commitment to work with others to do something about it?

2. What are our motives? Is this just a good idea that sparks our interest, or is God really calling us to become involved? What would Jesus do? Even more pertinently, what would Jesus, knowing us, want us to do?

3. How much time and energy is the campaign likely to involve? Do I/we have the time and energy for this? What about our other commitments?

4. If I'm in school, have a job, or have family obligations, who will take over my responsibilities if participation in the campaign means I can't keep my regular schedule? (Those who stay back and cover for you are just as important as the activists. Don't leave them in the lurch.)

Discernment doesn't stop once you've decided to become part of the campaign. Keep thinking and praying all along the way to discern whether God is *continuing* to call you in this direction. "Test the spirits to see if they are of God" (1 John 4:1). "If we live by the Spirit, let us also be guided by the Spirit" (Gal. 5:25).

Fr. John Dear, SJ, put it well: "In committing ourselves to nonviolence, we must act, reflect, study, and share with one another, but always listen to God and hear in what direction we are being called."[3]

Or, as Monica Brown wrote in her book *Embodying the God We Proclaim*, "Perhaps the beginning point is in listening; listening to that stirring [of the Spirit] within us, attending to the movement of grace that searches and questions, that wonders and marvels at the possibilities it senses."[4]

# Step 2:
# Prepare Spiritually

As the Church always has taught, Jesus is "the way, the truth, and the life" (John 14:6). Abiding in Christ's love (John 14:21–23; 15:1–14), we can receive the compassion, guidance, courage, and strength to walk the path of gospel nonviolence. "Apart from me you can do nothing," said Jesus (John 15:5). True gospel nonviolence is only possible, in the words of the liturgical prayer, "through him, with him, and in him." As we are nurtured by the body and blood of Christ in the Eucharist, we too can become bread broken and wine poured out for others.

Jesus asks us to love not only one another but our enemies as well. Our ability to meet this high standard depends, not only on our own desire to follow him, but even more on God's Spirit acting within us. We are not saints, but every practitioner of gospel nonviolence and every group committed to it would do well to spend time in prayer and worship to become more open to God's Spirit. We do this "because love is from God" and, as we love others, "God's love is perfected in us" (1 John 4:7, 12). We do this because, in a campaign for church reform, our "enemies" will normally be fellow Christians who oppose what we're about.

We who are committed to church reform have important talents, but like all humans we also are weak and fallible. Therefore, we need to lean prayerfully on Jesus, not only at the initiation of a nonviolent campaign, but at every step of the way. When we do not live up to our potential and make mistakes, we turn to him for forgiveness, and begin again.

## ANGER IN GOSPEL NONVIOLENCE

Dealing with our anger is a special challenge we face in building a Christ-centered nonviolent campaign. Because this is such a crucial issue for many of us wounded by the Catholic Church, it needs thoughtful, careful examination.

Many Catholics feel not only sadness, but also enormous (and justified) outrage at the behavior of Church leaders, such as priests who abused innocent children, and bishops covering up abuse. Many have been deeply hurt by the Church—sometimes by sexual abuse, but also by treatment that doesn't honor their adulthood, experience, intelligence, or gifts. Others' anger comes from a sense of helplessness at their frustrated attempts to change the Church. For some Catholics, this anger is so deep that they can see almost nothing good in the Church. They make sweeping and scornful generalizations about Church leaders and have trouble seeing anything redeeming in them. They can call them, as a Catholic activist said recently, "those fascists in clerical collars." Even Catholics who don't carry such bristling outrage can fall into generalizing about Church leaders or find themselves referring to them with disdain. Such leaders can come to be seen, not as individuals with a range of experiences and opinions, but as an amorphous, scowling, closed-minded "they." Direct action carried out in such a spirit, says Sr. Mary Lou Kownacki, "runs the risk of being superficial or worse—hypocritical, masking deep hostility, self-righteousness, and a desire to defeat and humiliate others."[5]

However tempting it is to give in to such unleashed outrage, if we lose sight of the humanity of others and their ability to change for the better, we are no longer being nonviolent. If we forget the presence of Christ in others, even those opposed to us, what we call "nonviolence" can become a vehicle for what St. Paul described as "enmities, strife, jealousy, anger, quarrels, dissensions" (Gal. 5:20). These can wound a Christian community and even tear it apart.

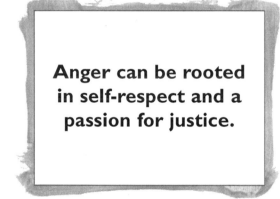

**Anger can be rooted in self-respect and a passion for justice.**

Overblown anger also can drive away possible supporters, including potentially sympathetic priests and bishops. These possible allies might be drawn to our reforms, were it not for their discomfort with the level of our rage and our apparent inability to recognize anything good in the Church or its leaders.

In light of this, it may be surprising to hear that a nonviolent approach does *not* rule out anger. Anger and love are not at opposite poles. Jesus himself knew righteous anger. For example, when confronted with religious leaders who used his healing on the Sabbath as a pretext for plotting his death, Jesus is described as "looking around at them in anger, grieved at their hardness of heart" (Mark 3:5).[6] St. Augustine related hope to anger when he wrote: "Hope has two lovely daughters, anger and courage; anger that things are not what they ought to be, courage to make them what they might be." Anger can be rooted in self-respect and a passion for justice.

Anger in gospel nonviolence, however, must always be at the service of love. As Catholic lay leader Sharon Browning once commented, "The issue is not anger, but what we do with it."[7] The Rev. James Bevel, a top member of Dr. King's staff, put it well when he said: "Be angry, but let your anger fuel your intelligence." That is, make intelligent, faithful, loving choices even in the midst of feeling angry. Let anger's energy inspire you to find nonviolent solutions. Hate the sin, but not the sinner. As St. Paul advised, "Be angry, but do not sin; do not let the sun go down on your anger" (Eph. 4:26). In other words, anger is sometimes inevitable. However, it must not trump our more basic obligation—to be reconciled with all, especially our brothers and sisters in the Christian community. "Be kind to one another, tenderhearted, forgiving one another as God in Christ has forgiven you" (Eph. 4:32).

We may not always be successful in placing our anger at the service of love. Certainly, we will fail at times, as a campaign unfolds, to realize the nonviolent ideal. The key question is, "Am I willing to start over and to do my best to grow into a loving, nonviolent spirit?"

## HOW CAN WE RESIST A SPIRIT OF INNER VIOLENCE?

Gospel nonviolence makes unusual demands on its practitioners. As Dr. Martin Luther King Jr. pointed out, "It avoids not only external physical violence but also internal violence of the spirit."[8] He expounds on the ways nonviolence chooses love instead of hate. It is willing to suffer, believing that unearned suffering is redemptive. It works to defeat injustice, not people. "The end is redemption and reconciliation," he concludes. "The aftermath of nonviolence is the creation of the beloved community."[9]

Jesus commands us to love our enemies. One reason this seems very hard, even impossible, is that, for us, the word *love* normally means feeling affection for someone and being drawn to them. How can we have affection for those who oppose us every step of the way? As Dr. King said: "We should be happy that Jesus did not say, '*Like* your enemies.' It is almost impossible to like some people . . . How can we be affectionate toward a person whose avowed aim is to crush our very being and to place innumerable stumbling blocks in our path . . . But Jesus recognized that *love* is greater than *like*."[10]

**The Christ**      *Jane E. Pitz*

Dr. King came to this conclusion through his biblical studies. What does the word *love* actually mean in the New Testament, he wondered? What does Jesus mean when he commands us to love our enemies? Is this just a sentimental, impossible ideal?

The New Testament, King learned, is fond of the word *love*, using it more than three hundred times. But the Greek language in which the New Testament was written includes three different words that are translated as *love* in English: *eros, philia,* and *agape.* The word *eros,* which connotes sexual or romantic love, is never found in the New Testament. The word *philia* (the affectionate love between friends) is used only 19 times. But the word *agape* appears 319 times. This is the word Jesus uses when he commands, "Love your enemies." Whereas *eros* and *philia* involve emotions and back-and-forth reciprocity between people, *agape* has nothing reciprocal, sentimental or affectionate about it. It means goodwill. It involves choice, not feelings. It is a decision to express goodwill toward an opponent, regardless of their response. It reaches out to the other, seeking nothing in return.[11] In *agape*, we love people because they are God's children whom God loves, just as God loves us. *Agape* separates the person from their evil deeds and goes out to them as a child of God. We love the person who does the evil deed while hating and opposing their evil acts. To Dr. King, it was extremely liberating to realize that loving the enemy carries no obligation to *like* the enemy.

This makes loving opponents still difficult—but less daunting. We don't have to like them. With God's help, we can find practical ways to "do good to those who hate you, bless those who curse you, pray for those who abuse you" (Luke 6:27–28). It is a love that becomes possible with God's help, because it is like God's own love, which "shines on the evil and the good, . . . the just and the unjust (Matt. 5:45). With God's love in our hearts, we can learn to follow St. Paul's instruction, "If your enemies are hungry, feed them; if they are thirsty, give them something to drink" (Rom. 12:20).

Nonviolent campaign-building gives us a way to channel our righteous anger into effective change without the destructiveness of hatred and hostility. And, as we will see in the pages ahead, active nonviolence gives us not only a positive spirit, but dozens of methods and specific steps to follow to build effective campaigns. Appendix 1 gives a number of exercises and meditations to help individuals and groups reflect on and grow more deeply into the nonviolent spirit of our enemy-loving God.

# Step 3:
# Organize Your Group

At the center of the best nonviolent action is a core of people who are committed to one another and to overcoming the injustice or oppressive situation in question. Shaping such a core is critical, demanding work. People need to be invited in. There may be disagreements at times, but as far as possible, everyone needs to work together around common goals. In your geographical area, either a direct-action group is still to be formed, is in the process of being formed, or has already come together. In whatever stage you're in, the material below should help you to strengthen your group.

An initial group may be only a few people. Jesus said, "Wherever two or three are gathered in my name, I am there among them." Rarely is it good to have more than ten or twelve people in the early stages, as this is a time for searching together, developing group cohesion and purpose, and defining tentative goals and strategies. When clarity of direction has been achieved, more people can be drawn in.

## INVOLVING NEW MEMBERS

**List:** Make a list of potentially interested individuals and groups and contact them. Whenever possible, approach people directly so you can explain personally what you have in mind. Potential group members might include: friends, church members, or members of existing peace and justice, reform, or social action groups. *(An effective way to invite others in is covered by the "One-on-One" method, described on page 53.)*

**DESCRIBE:** Create a leaflet or make copies of an article that highlights the issue your group will address. Pass them out. Ask people for reactions and see if they would like to do something about it.

**MEET:** Reserve space and then announce at Church that there will be a meeting after Mass to discuss the issue. Anyone interested is invited. Sometimes having an outside speaker or a film is a draw.

**ORGANIZE:** If you're already part of another group, invite group members to join your campaign. If their whole group doesn't want to participate, ask if you can form a "Direct Action" or "Gospel Nonviolence Committee" for those who would like to join your campaign but would prefer to stay under the auspices of their group.

## KEEP THINGS STRAIGHT WITH A NOTEBOOK

Some people try to organize direct action out of their hip pocket. They jot down phone numbers on slips of paper that get lost. They forget what the group decided three meetings ago. Organize your information. Use a looseleaf notebook, divided into sections like: "Meeting Notes," "Member Names, Phones, and E-mails," "Press Contacts," "Strategy Ideas," "Information on the Issue." This will help keep track of group decisions and the names of the many people who flow through a direct-action campaign.

## FOSTER A POSITIVE GROUP SPIRIT

1. **RESPECT YOUR MEMBERS:** Start and end meetings on time. Make people feel welcome. Begin meetings with introductions. When possible, serve refreshments. Contact new people to encourage them to come back. Pray at the beginning and end of each meeting—and also to ask God's guidance during the meeting.

2. **MEETING GUIDELINES OR AGREEMENTS:** Agree on guidelines for the conduct of your meetings. Guidelines might include:

   *We will—*

   ✢ Do our best to create a prayerful spirit in our meetings.

   ✢ Not interrupt when someone else is speaking.

   ✢ Be careful not to dominate the meeting if we tend to be more vocal than others.

   ✢ Encourage participation by trying to include quieter people in the discussion, but also respect those who prefer just to listen.

   ✢ Keep our meetings focused by sticking to the agenda and avoiding long tangents.

   ✢ Take our share of responsibility for the group's work and follow through on commitments.

3. **AGENDA:** To keep down chaos and wandering off the subject, have a written agenda for meetings. At the beginning of the meeting, do an agenda review to see if others have additional ideas they think need to be discussed. At the end of the meeting, ask people what should go on the next meeting's agenda. Leave time for prayer.

4. **FACILITATION AND MINUTES:** Have a designated facilitator for each meeting. The facilitator presents the agenda and keeps the group on task during the meeting. If certain members of the group are particularly gifted at facilitation, you might ask those people to facilitate every meeting. Or you can rotate facilitation among everyone who is willing. Be sure to choose a minute-taker for each meeting (permanent or rotated) so you will have a record of decisions, plans, and commitments.

5. **NEWSPRINT PAD:** Often it's helpful to use a flip chart to write down things like group agreements, jobs to be done, and responsibilities. This gives a sense of clarity, accomplishment, and forward motion to the group. People can see agenda items being ticked off, responsibilities being assumed, good ideas being noted, etc.

6. **EVALUATION:** To improve the quality and effectiveness of meetings, do a brief evaluation at the end. Only two questions need to be asked: What did we do well at this meeting? What could we do even better at our next meeting?

7. **ENJOY:** Serve refreshments. Celebrate. Sing. Dance. Affirm one another. Throw a potluck.

## DIVIDE THE WORK

In the early stages of group formation, everyone may do just about everything. As the work begins to pile up and the group grows larger, divide the labor. Set up committees and assign specific roles based on members' talents, interests, and leadership ability. For example, you probably will want to form a Coordinating or Executive Committee to give oversight to the whole operation. Outreach, Research, Fundraising, and Press Relations are some other committee possibilities. Important roles are chair or co-chair (spokesperson, meeting facilitator), secretary (keeps minutes and correspondence), treasurer (financial records), prayer facilitator (ensures that prayer opens and closes meetings). Add committees as needed.

## HANDLE DISAGREEMENTS CREATIVELY

Since people are so diverse, we can assume there will be disagreements. Keep in mind that conflict is not un-Christian nor is it something to be avoided at all costs. (See Acts 15 for creative ways the early Church handled conflict.) Here are some things to keep in mind and to say if disagreement or real conflict erupts.

**Conflict is an opportunity to go deeper.** *"Let's have as many different perspectives on this as we can. Before we can agree, we have to take some time to look at all sides of this."*

**Separate issues and people.** *"Sure, we disagree on this, but our relationship is a lot more important than our disagreement."*

**Handle conflict directly** and avoid talking about others behind their backs. *"I'm feeling confused and upset about our discussion—I'd really like to sit down and talk with you."*

**Don't equate your opinion with the will of God!** *"I have a little different take on this, but I respect your views and will think about them."*

**Really listen to what the other is saying.** *"So the way you see it, then, it would be best to . . . "*

# Deepen Your Nonviolent Commitment

1. Your group may draw people with no experience in active nonviolence. Some may have doubts about their ability to practice nonviolence. Even people with experience can always deepen their understanding and commitment. Suggestions:

   ✠ Review Step 2 in this chapter and Appendix 1 (see page 125). They suggest many ways to deal creatively with anger, learn how to love enemies, and to live out nonviolence.

   ✠ Study together a book by Dr. Martin Luther King Jr. or Mahatma Gandhi.

   ✠ Rent and watch a film on nonviolence. The movie *Gandhi* is an inspiring masterpiece. The two-video set *A Force More Powerful: A Century of Nonviolent Conflict* shows many examples of nonviolent movements. It has its own study guide and companion book by the same title.

   ✠ Pray together for a deeper understanding of and commitment to the spirituality of nonviolence.

2. Don't argue too much about the philosophy or theology of nonviolence. Look upon it not only as a mandate of the gospel but as perhaps the most effective strategy to achieve our goals. A nonviolent orientation often comes from answering the question, "Will this particular tactic help or hinder us in achieving our goals?"

## Step 4:
# Investigate

Gandhi used the word *satyagraha*—firmly grasping the truth—to describe his direct-action campaigns. During your group's nonviolent campaign, members will be called upon by the press or interested people to articulate why your group is focusing on this particular issue. If a listener or opponent can point out that your facts or interpretations are clearly incorrect, the campaign stalls right there. No one will support a campaign whose organizers haven't taken the trouble to learn the facts surrounding the issue in question. So be prepared. Investigate. Do research. Don't get "caught with your facts down."

## OPENNESS AND UNDERSTANDING

Inform yourself on all the arguments *against* the position your group is taking. You may be tempted to dismiss offhandedly a particular position taken by Church leadership as "nothing more than their attempt to shore up clerical power." However, if they publicly offer convincing reasons for their position, you must be prepared to respond.

# Some Research Methods

**INTERVIEWS:** Prepare a list of pertinent questions and interview people who know about the issue, including people purported to be experts. Don't rule out people who may be "part of the problem."

**MEDIA AND INTERNET SEARCHES:** Look up articles in magazines and newspapers as well as doing extensive searches in electronic sources.

**ORGANIZATIONS:** What organizations may have important information on the issue? Do they have newsletters, a library, or a website?

**REPORTERS:** Have any reporters been covering the issue? See if you can meet with them.

**LIBRARY RESEARCH:** Enlist researching tips from staff at local public and institutional libraries.

**RESOURCE FILE:** Collect information on the topic in a file that's accessible to group members for use in speaking engagements, press releases, and other occasions.

This means you need to do the sometimes daunting work of actually reading Vatican documents or talking to Church officials to try to understand their reasoning. As Vatican expert and *NCR* reporter John L. Allen Jr. says: "If one wishes to challenge [a Church policy], that challenge will be more effective if one can show how an alternative strategy could better serve the legitimate values the Holy See is trying to uphold, rather than just scolding the Vatican for arrogance."[12] Remember, you and your group are very well-informed (in fact, you are experts) on a crucial piece of Catholicism—what it means to be a lay Catholic.

Go one step further and try honestly to be open to any truth in the opposing position. (Usually, there's at least *some* truth on both sides.) Never make the arrogant claim that "only our way is right." Be open to being convinced that part of your position was inadequate or wrong. Make changes accordingly.

## PLAY "OUR SIDE, THE OTHER SIDE"

How can you know if you've really understood what "the other side" thinks? How can you see if you have good responses to their arguments?

Try this. Form two groups of two or three people. One group represents your position. The other represents those who oppose what you're doing. Imagine a meeting where each side has come to argue its own stance. For example, your side says Church leaders should be transparent about Church finances. The other side thinks that's a really bad idea.

Allow each side to take five or ten minutes to prepare: Who will speak first? What are the main points they want to make? Then have the two sides debate, with others as observers. Stop after ten or fifteen minutes.

When the discussion is over, ask participants how it felt to be in their respective roles, what information was new to them, and what arguments were most persuasive. Let observers comment on how well the participants did in stating your group's position and that of the other side. The arguments your side had trouble answering may suggest areas where you need to do more research.

## LOOK FOR ALTERNATIVE SOLUTIONS

It's not enough to have a clear idea of what's wrong. You also need to be able to propose how the wrong could be made right. Seek to offer reasonable suggestions for how things can be done better. People are more likely to join the campaign if they see not only the injustice, but how things could be done more justly.

## DON'T GET STUCK HERE!

Beware of "paralysis by analysis." Research can become an excuse for inaction. Gather the facts you need, but move ahead when you judge that you have a basic grasp of the issue. In any case, "investigation" doesn't screech to a halt as you move to the later steps. It should be ongoing. There always will be new things to learn that suggest new directions for your campaign.

# Step 5:
# Strategize

**B**efore initiating the 1963 nonviolent movement to integrate Birmingham, Alabama, Dr. King met with his aides and advisors for a three-day retreat to strategize and develop a detailed plan for the campaign. In it, they set the goal of activating the entire Black community and bringing about the integration of all the city's public facilities. Their overall strategy was to put pressure on merchants, using the tactics of boycotts, marches, and sit-ins. This was their basic "strategic plan."[13]

A strategic plan specifies the general course of action selected to achieve your goals. According to Gene Sharp, to *strategize* is to think through the steps needed "to make it more likely to get from the present to a desired future situation."[14] The basic questions a plan must address are: Where are we? Where do we want to go? Why? How can we get there?

Not every campaign requires a detailed, written strategic plan. A written plan, or something like it, however, can be a helpful tool for developing a strong campaign. Because strategic planning is often neglected (to the detriment of nonviolent movement-building) we will discuss this concept in some detail. While strategic plans often vary in their details, most plans include the following five items:[15]

**VISION**
**VALUES**
**GOALS**
**ASSESSMENT**
**ACTION PLAN**

Let's look at how these five pieces might come together in a typical campaign. For this example, we'll take a situation that could be true in any number of dioceses. Let's say that in your diocese, the bishop resides in an opulent mansion costing millions of dollars. Here he lives a princely lifestyle with a retinue of cooks, gardeners, chauffeurs, and housekeepers. Your group wants to address the opulence of this lifestyle in contrast to the needs of the poor in your region. We will use this situation to illustrate our discussion of strategic planning and campaign building.

## STATE YOUR VISION

Decide where you're headed. Ask yourself: What is the aim of our campaign? What do we hope will be different in the future as a result of what we do? What do we want the future to look like? What change, if achieved, would let us say, "Our campaign has been a success?" Try to state this vision clearly and simply, so that it can be written down in one or two brief sentences. In such a case, you might write:

*VISION STATEMENT: Our vision is of a diocese in which our bishop lives simply, more like Jesus did. Rather than living in a palatial mansion, the bishop would live in a modest, inner-city apartment, and the mansion would be sold, with its proceeds used to strengthen the Church's work on behalf of the poor.*

## STATE YOUR VALUES

Sit back for a minute and think: What is motivating us to start this campaign? Why are we concerned? What are the values that underlie our commitment? How does our faith influence what we want to do?

Having your values clearly in mind serves three purposes: (1) Doing so keeps you focused; (2) When the going gets tough, it helps remind you of the importance of what you're doing and it motivates you to keep at it; (3) When others ask, "Why are you doing this?" (as they inevitably will), having your values on the tip of your tongue gives you a strong, clear answer. Here are some values underlying our example:

1. **WE BELIEVE OUR BISHOPS SHOULD FOLLOW JESUS:** Church leaders, including our bishop, should model their lives on Jesus, who warned about the danger of wealth (Matt. 6:24; 19:23–25), lived simply (Luke 9:58), and called his followers to do the same (Luke 12:15, 33). An ostentatious lifestyle is contrary to the example and teachings of Jesus.

2. **OUR OWN CATHOLIC CHURCH TEACHES THAT BISHOPS SHOULD LIVE SIMPLY:** Canon 387 of the *Code of Canon Law* mandates that bishops practice "simplicity of life." The Vatican's *Directory for the Pastoral Ministry of Bishops* says each bishop should "be poor and appear to be poor." On a trip to the United States, Pope John Paul II told U.S. bishops they should adopt a lifestyle that "imitates the poverty of Christ" so the Church can better identify with the struggles and suf-fering of the poor.[16]

The Bishop's Palace of Galveston, Texas has an estimated value of 5.5 million.

3. **HISTORICAL PRECEDENTS:** Long ago, St. Gregory the Great (pope from AD 590–604) turned his Roman hilltop palace into a Benedictine house of prayer. In 2003, Boston's new archbishop, Sean O'Malley, decided to live modestly in a South Boston rectory, shunning the grandiose bishop's residence . There are many examples, ancient and modern, of bishops who have lived simply and close to their people.

## SET CLEAR GOALS

Goals are your aims, where you need to go to realize your vision and values. They are general statements, usually without reference to the specifics of what, when, who, or how. They are not as concrete as objectives (which we'll describe in a minute), but they should be specific enough to suggest what action is needed to reach them. "To make Church leaders live more like Christ" may be a great goal, but it's too general to be an action focus. Concrete campaign goals might be:

1. To get our bishop to move from the mansion to a simpler residence.

2. To encourage Church leaders to sell the mansion and use the proceeds to help the poor.

3. To rally local Catholics to join us or to take their own action toward those ends.

As is the case with values, knowing your goals helps your group stay focused and explain your campaign to others. It also helps you evaluate what's being accomplished. "Are we realizing our goals or not?"

## DO A STRATEGIC ASSESSMENT

Having stated your vision and goals, make a realistic assessment of how likely you are to reach them. What are you up against? How prepared are you to overcome the opposition you will face? What are your strengths and weaknesses? On whom will you need to bring nonviolent pressure to create change?

The acronym **SWOT** can help you remember what goes into an assessment.

**S - Strengths**: What are our group's strengths? What strong points will help us achieve our goals?

**W - Weaknesses**: What are our weaknesses? What areas do we need to shore up to achieve our goals?

**O - Opportunities**: What opportunities can we take advantage of?

**T - Threats**: What forces will try to hinder us from attaining our goals?

Before setting out on the campaign, **SWOT** will help you consider how to build on your group's strengths, buttress its weaknesses, make the best use of opportunities, and prepare to respond to forces opposing you. (For more questions to help in your assessment, see Appendix 3, "Questions for a Strategic Assessment.")

Using our mansion example, here's how your SWOT might read: **Strengths:** We are highly committed—members feel strongly about the contrast between our bishop's lifestyle and the teachings of Jesus and the Church. In addition, there is broad potential support for our goals, since 74 percent of ordinary Catholics believe our bishop should live more like Christ. **Weaknesses:** We are all busy and wonder if we can find the time necessary to work on our campaign. Our support from ordinary Catholics is only potential, since we haven't found an effective way to communicate with more than a few of them. **Opportunity:** We can invite a media professional to explain how to strengthen our outreach to the public through TV, the press, and other venues. **Threat:** The diocese has a paid public-relations staff who may well use the media to try to discredit us.

## IDENTIFY THE FINAL DECISION-MAKERS

Another crucial part of your strategic assessment is to figure out where the buck stops. Somewhere, there is a person (or a small group of people) who has the authority to say whether the change will be made or not. These final decision-makers are the targets of your action. In Catholic governance, this usually is a single person—the local bishop. In our illustration, he has the power to decide if he will stay in the mansion. In other cases, a group of officials may share this power.

These final decision-makers are usually surrounded by gatekeepers—layers of staff who obey them and control access to them. In most cases, the gatekeeper will try to keep you from getting to the real power-holders. They may meet with you intending to keep you at the gate. You may need to do a lot of groundwork and rallying of the troops to get past these folks. But, finally, you do need to get past them. If you don't, the change won't happen.

Specifying the real power-holders keeps your campaign focused, with your main energies aimed at reaching and influencing those who can bring about the change you want.

## DRAW UP AN ACTION PLAN

The action plan lays out what you need to do to reach your goals. Once you've set goals and done an assessment, it is probable that you will see a number of possible ways of reaching those goals. To narrow these, decide on your specific plan, including the objectives and tactics you will use.

### I. Agree on a General Statement of Your Action Plan

You first need to craft a statement detailing your plan. It should not be more than a few sentences long. As an illustration: "To pursue our three goals, we will first try to meet with our bishop. If we can arrange a meeting, we will present him with our best arguments for why he should move out of the mansion and into a modest apartment. If we are not able to meet with him, we will initiate a nonviolent, direct-action campaign to persuade him to move."

## 2. Specify Your Objectives

Objectives describe the results you intend to achieve. They are the targets at which you must aim to accomplish your goals. They are much more specific than goals. Each objective contains WHAT you want to happen, WHEN you want it to happen, and WHO will work to make it happen. While there are only a few goals, which are generally stated, there can be many objectives. **SAM** is an acronym you can use to remember what goes into each objective.

**S - Specific:** It is clearly worded and easy to understand, stating clearly what you want, the date by which you intend to achieve it, and the person(s) who have primary responsibility for working on it.

**A - Attainable**: It is doable—a statement of the possible. Your group, alone or in cooperation with others, has the power to bring about. It's not pie in the sky.

**M - Measurable**: It is stated in such a way that you can easily determine whether you've achieved it or not.

## Example of objectives:

a. *By June,* our *Research Team* will collect as much information as possible about the mansion.

b. Also *by June,* our *Negotiation Team* will meet with selected clergy and diocesan officials to hear their rationale for maintaining such a luxurious residence. (This will help us further prepare our arguments.)

c. *By July,* our *Secretary* will send our new bishop an initial letter asking to meet with him to discuss why we think he should move out of the mansion.

d. *By August,* if we have not heard from the bishop, our *Executive Committee* will develop a plan of nonviolent action to achieve our goals.

e. Also *by August,* our *Executive Committee* will send the bishop a second, more detailed letter stating our case for moving out of the mansion and the nonviolent campaign we will initiate. Our *Press Committee* will hold a press conference and circulate our letter to the media to announce our nonviolent campaign.

f. *During September,* our *Education Committee* will organize a large meeting of all interested laity to explain our action plan and to invite their participation. Press will be invited to attend.

g. *By October,* we will take the first step of direct action, led by our *Direct Action Committee.*

h. *From beginning to end,* our *Finance Committee* will develop a budget and fund-raising methods to finance each step of the campaign.

### 3. Direct-Action Methods

In all likelihood, you will not embark on direct action (prayer vigils, demonstrations, etc.) at the very beginning of your campaign. First, you probably will want to make a good-faith effort to convince power-holders (through negotiations) that what you are proposing is reasonable, necessary, and flows from our common faith. However, when you dialogue and first formulate your strategic plan, it is important to begin thinking about the nonviolent direct-action methods available to you and which ones may be most appropriate to achieve your campaign goals.

At this point, planners will want to review Chapter 4, "The Many Methods of Active Nonviolence." It describes 80 specific direct-action methods, with 190 examples of how these methods have been used in the past. It also gives many ideas for how particular methods could be used today. Almost certainly some of these will be applicable to your campaign; others may not be. As you consider which methods to use, a key question is: "Would this method advance us toward our goals and objectives?" For more details on how to plan a direct action, see Steps 8 to 11, pages 56–69.

## A FINAL NOTE ON STRATEGY

You will need to revise your strategic plan as the campaign unfolds. New and unanticipated situations may arise. What looked good on paper may not be so good in practice. One advantage of the strategic planning method is that it allows its users to clearly articulate its vision, goals, and strategy so they can be updated as new circumstances require. Feel free to change the wording of goals, add new objectives, or make any other revisions that keep your planning in touch with the reality you are facing.

This faith-based vigil against the Iraq war was organized by Sojourners
on the fourth anniversary of the war.
*Photo by Ryan Rodrick Beiler, courtesy of www.sojo.net*

 # Step 6:
# Negotiate

## THE IMPORTANCE OF NEGOTIATIONS

Some activists get fired up about hitting the streets, as if demonstrations are the only way to be serious. Remember: our purpose is to correct a wrong, not to prove our courage. If you can accomplish your purpose without demonstrations (and without making unwarranted concessions), then negotiations are an excellent way to go.

Steps 1 to 6 are not meant to create a slippery slope leading inevitably to confrontation through direct action. Gandhi and Dr. King both said frequently that they would much prefer to settle with their opponents through negotiation rather than having to use demonstrations. Committed to love and truth, they saw their actions as a way, not to "win over" (defeat) their opponents, but to "win them over." They believed God can soften even the hardest of hearts. They didn't want to humiliate the power-holders. They looked for ways to let the decision-makers save face. Without being naive or compromising basic principles, they looked for ways both sides could win.

## WHEN—AND WITH WHOM—TO NEGOTIATE

We are labeling negotiations as Step 6, but in reality they can happen at any point in a campaign. For example, they may happen early on if power-holders get wind of what you're doing and ask for a meeting to sound you out. Or negotiations may happen when you start poking around in your Step 4 investigations. Or at Step 11, when power-holders realize negotiations are preferable to facing direct action.

Most likely, though, they will happen at your initiative after your group has done research, chosen an issue, and formed an initial strategy to address it. Since you're seeking change, you will want to talk to the person or persons who have the power to make the change. In our illustration, for example, the issue could be resolved if you could meet with the bishop and convince him to live in an inner-city apartment rather than the plush residence.

The question of whom to negotiate with is crucial. If you're dealing with a hierarchical structure, it's unlikely that you'll easily get an appointment with those who actually have power to make the needed changes. More likely, if you can get a meeting at all, a lower-level gatekeeper will be assigned to meet with you. If this happens, ask the person whether they have authority to make the change. If they do not, you might politely decline to meet with him or her, saying that you really need to meet with those in charge. The primary value in meeting with such persons is to get a sense of the arguments power-holders may use and to hone your group's negotiation skills. You may also gain an advocate on the inside. If you do meet at this lower level, be sure to make clear that you intend to go higher up.

## HOW TO GET NEGOTIATIONS GOING

Most of our reform and renewal groups are relatively small and have few resources. It's easier for authorities to stonewall us than agree to meet with us. Therefore, your group may need to do a build-up to encourage negotiations. Send a letter requesting a meeting by certified mail (so they can't say, "We never received it.") Or, send the letter with someone (a sympathetic priest?) who can deliver it personally and encourage a reply. If you get innocuous replies—or none—try writing an open letter and see if you can get it published in the newspaper.

If these methods are unsuccessful, send a final letter stating your commitment to direct action if there is no response by such and such a date. If they continue to ignore you, hold a press conference to explain your campaign, express your disappointment, and publicly request a meeting. If stonewalling continues, you will need to move to Steps 7 to 11 of this process, while remaining open to negotiation if an opportunity opens after direct actions have begun.

## IF NEGOTIATIONS OCCUR

Don't just dive into talks. If you don't prepare ahead of time, you may easily to be taken in by vague promises, friendly but evasive statements, or public-relations snow jobs. The story is told of the Kennedys inviting the children of civil-rights leaders to the White House. The kids were fired up. They proudly told their parents of the tough demands for freedom and equality they would make to these powerful leaders. When they returned, their parents asked, "How did the White House respond?" They replied that they really hadn't had a chance to voice their proposals. When asked why, they said, "Well, the Kennedys were really nice, and they had a lot of ice cream and sodas all laid out for us, so we sort of forgot . . . "

President Lyndon B. Johnson meets with civil rights leaders Martin Luther King Jr., Whitney Young, and James Farmer.
*Photo by Yoichi R. Okamoto, 1964*

Unless they are seriously interested in talks, power-holders will just want to brush you off. Most dioceses have staff who are skilled at handling complaints from parishioners. Other dioceses have access to professionals in public relations. A favorite approach for gatekeepers is to be very friendly, thank the group for coming, serve coffee, listen carefully, take notes, talk about the importance of continued dialogue, but commit to *nothing*. Many a negotiation team has come away from such a meeting believing they made progress, when in reality they departed from the meeting empty-handed.

## PREPARATIONS TO MAKE WELL BEFORE THE NEGOTIATION SESSION

### Be Clear about Your Goals

To avoid being taken in by such tactics, groups should prepare extremely carefully *before* any meeting with power-wielders. First, be clear about *what* you want to happen as a result of the meeting, *when* and *how* it will happen, and *who* will be responsible for making it happen. Write this down in two or three clear, unambiguous sentences. Make sure your whole group understands and agrees with the goals. Call it "What We Are Asking." Here's a goal statement that fits with our illustration:

## WHAT WE ARE ASKING

Because of the contradiction between the bishop's mansion and (1) the teachings and example of Christ, (2) the description of bishops' preferred lifestyle in the Code of Canon Law, and (3) the instructions in the Vatican's Directory for the Pastoral Ministry of Bishops, we are asking that:

1. Within the next month, the diocese put the mansion up for sale on the market, doing the necessary advertising to make sure potential buyers are aware of the sale.

2. Within the next month, our bishop publicly announce his agreement with this decision and seek modest living quarters in the inner city.

Discuss among yourselves whether your proposals are nonnegotiable or whether there's room for a compromise that won't be a sellout. If they're unwilling to accede completely to your proposals, could they make initial moves or commit to alternative timelines your group could accept as an indication of good faith? For example, regarding the "What We Are Asking" proposals above, would your group accept a compromise which says: "The diocese is not able to make a definite commitment to sell the mansion within a month, since we need to consult with the Diocesan Finance Council. However, we agree to propose this plan to them positively and to meet again with your group within a month"?

## Do a Role-play of the Expected Negotiation

It is one thing to discuss your proposal in the abstract. It is quite another to actually get a feel of what it will be like to present these ideas to a group of (probably unsympathetic) power-holders. The role-play provides that feel. It evokes emotions as well as ideas. It gives a realistic run-through of the negotiation prior to the real meeting. It gives your group a chance to see how your negotiators can present the group's proposals most effectively in the highly charged give-and-take of an actual negotiation. It gives insight into what the power-holders on the other side of the table are likely to be thinking and what strategies they may use in relating to your group.

Members of your group may say that role-plays are artificial. It's true that role-plays are not identical to the real situation. But they do simulate crucial aspects of reality so that important issues and approaches can be explored more fully than in verbal discussions.

President Lyndon B. Johnson signs the 1964 Civil Rights Act as Martin Luther King, Jr., and others look on.
*Photo by Cecil Stoughton*

# Role-Play

**a. PLAN YOUR ROLE-PLAY SCENARIO:** Develop your exercise based on your best guess of what your negotiators will face at their meeting. Important components are: (1) The scene where the negotiations take place, (2) The cast of characters, (3) Any special equipment (such as a table and chairs) that will be needed to make the exercise as realistic as possible.

**b. THE RIGHT ATTITUDE:** It's natural to be a little nervous when asked to perform in this way. People may be tempted not to take the exercise seriously. However, the more realistically you can play your roles, the more you will learn. Make clear at the outset that there's no wrong way to play a part. No one will be ridiculed or judged. No Oscars will be given.

**c. ASK FOR VOLUNTEERS:** You'll need a few volunteers to play the power-holders and the same number to play the negotiating team. All others are observers, and need to be very aware of words, body language, and the attitudes and feelings that emerge in the interaction.

**d. PREPARATION:** Give the two groups a few minutes to discuss how they will play their roles. Will the authorities group take a hard line or try the snow-job approach? Which of your negotiators will make the opening statement? Who will present the proposals? Who will play other roles?

**e. RUN THE ROLE-PLAY:** Allow the role-play to continue long enough to bring out the relevant issues. End it when a natural break occurs or when nothing new seems to be forthcoming. Don't let it run too long.

**f. EVALUATE:** ➤ Any spontaneous reactions? How does everyone feel? What happened? ➤ **Ask the power-wielders**: What power-plays did you attempt? Did you feel successful in holding off the negotiators? Did they say or do anything that got through to you? What was most effective? ➤ **Ask the negotiators**: How did it feel to play your role? What did you do right? Anything you wish you'd said or done differently? ➤ **Ask the observers**: Anything you especially noticed? Was the negotiation a success? Did the power-wielders respond specifically to the proposals? Did the negotiators convey an attitude of nonviolent respect and goodwill toward the authorities, without backing off on their proposals and their call for action? What could a group of negotiators do better next time? ➤ **In general**: What did we learn? What do we need to keep in mind for an actual negotiation session?

# KEEP THE PRESS INFORMED

It's likely that power-holders will want to meet quietly behind the scenes. "The press will just distort things," they're likely to say. However, unless there are very good reasons not to go to the press, it's a good practice to keep the media informed. This makes clear to the general public and Catholics at large that you're not an elite group that's afraid to have its processes see the light of day. Also, if power-holders know there will be press coverage, it can be an additional inducement to take the meeting seriously.

# PREPARATIONS JUST BEFORE THE NEGOTIATION SESSION

1. **DECISION-MAKERS:** As mentioned before, try to ensure you will talk with someone who has the authority to make the needed change when you first arrange the meeting.

2. **LENGTH OF THE MEETING:** Be sure you will have enough time to present and discuss your proposals and hear their response. You don't want to get into the predicament of having the power-holders say after ten minutes, "We're sorry, but we need to leave for an important meeting. So nice to meet you."

3. **CHOOSE A GROUP OF NEGOTIATORS:** Never send a "lone ranger" to negotiate. Always have a team of three or four. Team members can support one another, play different (but complementary) roles in the session, and more accurately report back what happened to the whole group. Be sure to pick people who complement one another and who are good negotiators (e.g., a parent with teenagers). Ask one of your members to take minutes of the meeting so you'll have a written record of discussions and decisions.

4. **AGREE ON ROLES:** Decide ahead of time which team members will handle which parts of the session.

## Key roles for a negotiation session

*Chair/Co-Chair:* Open the meeting, hand out the agenda, make sure you keep to it.

*Recorder:* Takes minutes.

*Prayer offerer:* Lead opening and closing prayer, and suggest prayer at any time during the meeting as needed. (You might also invite authorities to pray if they wish.)

*Proposer:* Explain what we are asking and why it is important. Invite their response.

*Closer:* (can be Coordinator) If you reach agreement, get a timeline for *what* the authorities will do, *when* and *how* they'll do it, and *who* will be responsible for carrying it out. If no agreement is reached, either get a date for another meeting or explain your group's commitment to public education and, if necessary, nonviolent direct action. Make clear your group is willing, at any point, to meet to answer questions or find a resolution.

5. **Type up an agenda:** *You* set the agenda. Hand out a printed one at the beginning of the meeting. Use polite but firm assertiveness to keep to it. (Power-holders are used to setting the agenda and may well want to impose their own plan for the meeting or steer the conversation away from substance and into small talk.)

6. **Pray:** Ask God for help. Pray that you will be calm, stick to your purpose, to be firm without being antagonistic, and practice *agape* love toward all concerned. Pray for those with whom you will be meeting, that God will open their minds and hearts to hear what you offer. Pray that your own heart will be open to their perspectives.

## Sample Agenda:

a. Introductions and lay-led prayer.

b. Hand out agenda.

c. Purpose of the meeting. Check in on the amount of time set aside.

d. What we are asking. Why our proposals are important.

e. What will resolve our concern. Response to our proposals.

f. Next steps: What, when, how, who?

g. Closing prayer.

## THE NEGOTIATION SESSION: KEY GUIDELINES

1. **Go as adult Catholics:** Church leaders tend to believe they know what's best. They may try to treat you like children who should be obedient. Because of our upbringing, it's easy to slip into a "Yes, Father" role. Resist infantilization. Be adult Catholics—with dignity, gifts, and intelligence. You have a right to make your views known. Challenging bishops or priests doesn't mean you don't respect or love them in Christ.

2. **Children of God:** Remember that you, and those with whom you are negotiating, are children of God. If they don't act like it, love them anyway. If you get mad and lose your cool, apologize.

3. **No confidential sessions:** Don't get drawn into secret or off-the-record negotiations. Make clear you're representing your group and need to report everything back to them.

4. **Stick to your agenda and assigned roles:** A certain amount of small talk is fine, but keep the conversation focused on your proposals. Don't get sidetracked. Stay in control of the meeting. Don't be afraid to raise uncomfortable questions. Be friendly and polite, but insist that the real issue be dealt with: Will the policy or practice be changed or not? If they can't give an immediate answer, ask for a date when you can meet again to get the answer. Inform them that you need to report such information back to your group and consider next steps.

5. **Get a firm answer:** Insist politely on a yes-or-no answer to your proposals. If no, why not?

6. **In writing:** If they agree verbally to your proposals, request a timetable for changes to be made. What, when, how, who? If possible, get it in writing. If that's not feasible, tell them you will send them a

written version of what you understand the agreement to be, requesting them to respond immediately if they had a different understanding.

7. **COUNTERPROPOSALS:** It's possible that your counterparts will make their own proposals. If theirs is to the point and not just a power play, listen sympathetically, but don't agree to anything other than what is in your proposal without a caucus: "Let's take a five-minute break for us to consider your idea."

8. **NEGOTIATIONS IN THE PLURAL:** Express willingness to continue negotiation meetings, but only if real progress is being made. Don't get drawn into a series of meetings that are an excuse for inaction. Often only one or two sessions will tell if this process is likely to be fruitful.

9. **CONSEQUENCES OF INACTION:** Don't threaten, but explain the nature of your direct-action group and its commitment to seeing the issue resolved. Make clear that if the problem can't be resolved through negotiations, your group is committed to public education and, if necessary, demonstrations in the spirit of gospel nonviolence.

## AFTER THE NEGOTIATION SESSION

1. **MINUTES:** Write an accurate summary of the meeting immediately.

2. **DEBRIEF:** Share the results with your group as soon as possible. What happened? Success? What did the team do right? What could they have done better? Next steps?

3. **PRESS RELATIONS:** Let your media contacts know what happened— by a press conference, if appropriate.

Press covering a civil-disobedience action in Bothell, Washington.

## Step 7:
# Educate and Build Broader Support

### WHY THIS STEP?

To some extent, your campaign will have been educating the public and building broader support all along. However, at Step 7, these efforts intensify greatly because either negotiations have broken down or power-holders have refused to negotiate at all. Now, you *are* on the path to direct action. Your goal now is to get more people to join you.

Suffragette with banner, Washington, D.C., 1918

The only reason to skip Step 7 is if you believe you can reach your vision with the people and resources who already have joined you. Very small groups can sometimes accomplish great things, but in most cases it's desirable to draw many more people into the campaign. Of course you need people who will join you in direct action. But you also need those who would never go near a demonstration but feel strongly enough about the issue that they'll talk to friends about it, write letters, raise money, or take other steps to support what you're doing. These people may not carry the "Where Would Jesus Live?" banner in front of the bishop's estate, but they might organize a letter-writing session after Mass where sympathetic people could send their views to the chancery. How can we reach such potential supporters?

### FRAME THE ISSUE SO IT APPEALS TO PEOPLE'S VALUES

Social change begins when enough people become increasingly uncomfortable because of a deep conflict between values they cherish on the one hand and some aspect of their current reality on the other. The tension between the two usually becomes more and more untenable. When people are offered a vision that resolves these intense moral conflicts, tremendous energy for change is released.

For over a century, women in the United States accepted with little effective protest that they could not vote. But outspoken suffragists, appealing to women's sense of dignity and equality and taking dramatic action to challenge the status quo, made them increasingly uncomfortable with their lack of full citizenship rights. They rallied millions of women (and their male allies) in a movement that abolished this second-class citizenship.

Technically, of course, the victory went to women of all races, but because of racial discrimination, White women were the primary beneficiaries. This moral tension became one of the seeds for another powerful and transformative social movement fifty years later, when hundreds of thousands of African Americans were joined by over sixty thousand Whites in freedom rides and other demonstrations. They could no longer bear the conflict between their values of human dignity and equal opportunity and the degrading, brutal treatment Blacks were suffering. The freedom movement offered them a way to act, and they embraced it.

Similarly, we must address our issue so people can see how some current reality contradicts their deeply-held values and can envision an alternative to an increasingly unacceptable status quo.

## DO ONE-ON-ONES

One-on-Ones are a way of doing outreach that have been very effectively used by Voice of the Faithful and other groups.[17] These are face-to-face conversations between two people that take place in about thirty to sixty minutes. The conversation explores their stories, interests, concerns, and resources. If possible, it results in a commitment. The purpose is to turn a list of names into a group of involved bodies. The advantage of this approach is that it's very personal. Many people are more likely to respond to an actual person than to an idea. They'll join the effort, not just because they're interested in the issue, but because they trust the person and think it could be fun to work with him or her.

### How to do One-on-Ones:

1. **Make a list:** Your direct-action group writes down the names of people you hope to involve in your campaign in some way. These can be friends, members of broader reform groups, allies in the community, or anyone else who might have interest. The list should include about five times as many names as the number of people who plan to make contact. Each member should contact about five people. Agree to make the calls within a specific time period and then get together to report back.

2. **Call:** Each of you calls the people on your list. The call is not to beg the other person to do what you're doing, an interview, or chitchat. It isn't an invitation to a gripe session about the Catholic Church. It is a personal, relationship-building, mutual-sharing conversation that will build sympathy and understanding

### Reach Out

Here are some methods of public education to try, depending on the population you want to reach and the skills of your group:

| | |
|---|---|
| Conferences | Statements by leaders |
| Public meetings | |
| Famous and/or inspiring speakers | Teach-ins |
| | Endorsements by celebrities |
| Home meetings | |
| Newspaper articles | Sermons |
| Op-Ed pieces | Leafleting |
| Letters to the Editor | Prayer meetings |
| | Website |
| Petitions | E-mails |
| Radio and TV interviews | Blogs |

Whenever you educate, always suggest something people can do to act on the issue. Write a letter. Organize a meeting in your parish. Invite a speaker. Provide financial support. Always give specific information, like the name and phone of a contact person, supplies and skills needed, and the date of the next direct action.

for what your group is doing and allow you to invite the person to join the group or support it in some other way.

3. **Practice** the conversation and questions in item 5 below with another member of your group.

4. **On the call:** When you reach the person, introduce yourself. Say that you're working with such and such a group and want to hear people's thinking on the issue you're concerned about. You'd like to meet for no more than an hour at the time and place of his or her choosing. You'd like to hear the concerns, ideas, and suggestions he or she may have.

5. **When you meet,** tell the person your story and ask her/him to share their own. Share your interests and concerns and solicit the same from him or her. Ask questions to probe what's on her/his mind and heart. Here are some ideas:

   ✛ *Where are you from originally?*

   ✛ *What did you study in school? Why?*

   ✛ *What do you do for a living?*

   ✛ *What do you feel strongly/passionately about?*

   ✛ *Who has influenced you most? How? Why do you look up to them?*

   ✛ *If there were one thing you could change about the Church, what would it be? Why?*

   ✛ *What do you think about the issue our group is addressing and how we're tackling it?*

   Don't trap your contact with a plea to get involved. Just say something like, "We're looking for new members for our group as we start the direct-action phase of our campaign. It sounds as though you have talents that would be helpful. Please don't feel any obligation to say yes, but if you'd be interested in working with our group, we'd love to talk about it more."

6. **Report:** Get back together in your group to share what happened in your interchanges. Decide what to do with this information—especially following up with anyone who expressed interest in joining your group.

## DO STREET SPEAKING

In street speaking, members of your group (having prepared ahead of time what to say) gather at some public place with lots of foot traffic. Bring a bullhorn or other amplification system. One after another, group members stand on a raised area (a sturdy box will do) and address passersby about your group's concerns. Other group members may hold posters or a banner. Others can hand out leaflets.

This is an excellent way to reach out to the public while at the same time getting your group's feet wet. Members who speak will be motivated to do their homework and really learn the facts about the issue. In order to get a positive response, they'll also have to reflect on why they got involved themselves. They'll have to think of provocative questions and challenging comments to spark the interest of passersby. They may even get experience with nonviolent means of handling hecklers!

## KEEP MOVING FORWARD

The period of public education and support-building can be long or short, depending on the situation. Avoid the temptation, however, to drag out the education forever. There are many instances in which the most effective public education will come through the kinds of direct action described in Chapter 4. Public meetings or sermons can go on for years and reach only a few hundred or a thousand people, while an effective series of demonstrations can reach millions of people through the mass media—putting direct pressure on those responsible for the wrong you're addressing.

The author and others in an anti-Vietnam war protest, blocking ammunition trains.
*Photo by Joseph Poindexter, 1972*

## Step 8:
# Prepare for Direct Action

The die is cast. You've done your best to dialogue with power-holders. They've either rebuffed your group entirely or met with you but made clear that more discussions won't move them. At this point, you have three choices: (1) Give up, (2) Keep using the same approach you've used so far, even though it's not working, (3) Try the stronger motivating methods direct action provides.

## MAKE A STRATEGIC ASSESSMENT

Before doing direct action, evaluate the strengths and weaknesses of your own group and of those who will use their power and influence to keep the status quo. Knowing this balance of forces can help you choose the most appropriate direct-action tactics for your situation. Your conclusions can be written down as a formal document, or it can just be discussed in your group. It can be time-consuming or not. Judge how useful you think it will be in your circumstances, then determine the format you will use and how much time and energy you will devote to it.

Any strategic estimate of power tries to answer the question, "Given our group's strengths and weaknesses and those of the power-holders, what is the likelihood that a direct-action campaign will be successful—or, if not completely successful, at least make a meaningful witness that will forward the cause?" Generally, it is not wise to move into major direct action if the campaign requires capacities beyond your group's current abilities—until, of course, those capacities are strengthened. Until then, direct action should take more limited forms that can make some impact without needing great strength.

Sometimes the results can look a bit scary. Success may seem highly unlikely, given the access power-holders have to major material resources and organizational strength, and their ability to apply sanctions. *But remember that most nonviolent movements throughout history have pitted apparently "weak" people and groups against those with seemingly far greater power.* What could look weaker than Jesus, hanging on a cross? History is full of the testimonies of groups which look very weak, but who successfully use powerful nonviolent approaches to confound the powers-that-be and bring about major change.

See Appendix 3 for a set of questions that you can use in your strategic assessment. (You may well think of other questions that apply to your specific situation.) Again, don't get bogged down. Do as much or as little as is helpful, and then move on. Pull out your assessment now and then and modify it as the situation changes and you gain more knowledge.

# CONSIDER THE
# DIRECT-ACTION POSSIBILITIES

Chapter 4 describes 80 different direct-action tactics. To illustrate these, the text provides 190 examples—from ancient times to the present—showing how people have applied these various approaches, usually with success. It also gives ideas for how the methods can be used today in Church reform.

As you read through, consider which methods would help your group put a spotlight on the injustice you're addressing. Which dramatizes the injustice so that many other people will understand the issue and want to do something to overcome the wrong? Which approaches would put pressure on power-holders so that, sooner rather than later, they make the required changes?

Keep in mind that a particular tactic or set of tactics will function best if used in the context of the overall strategy developed in Step 5.

## WRITE A "COVENANT OF NONVIOLENCE"

Successful nonviolent campaigns often have a written covenant or agreement that reminds demonstrators of their commitment to nonviolence. Passed out as a flyer at the time of the action, it also informs police, observers, and anyone joining the action of the demonstration's nonviolent spirit. It can be very simple, with points like:

**Jesus** *unknown artist*

✚ We will keep before us Jesus, the Prince of Peace.

✚ We will act with love, because "God is love" (1 John 4:8).

✚ We will be open, friendly, and respectful to all we meet.

✚ We will prayerfully stay in touch with our inner sources of truth and love.

✚ If we meet hostility, we will not respond in kind.

✚ We will follow the instructions of the designated coordinators. If we cannot, we will withdraw from the action.

# ORGANIZE FOR DIRECT ACTION

Once you've decided on the strategy and tactics you'll use, you need to organize so you can best carry out the campaign. The following list contains tasks that, ideally, need to be covered in every direct action. Usually, each is best carried out by a small group or team, though some can be performed by an individual. Often, people have responsibility for more than one task. Use the following twelve points as a checklist. Do the jobs appropriate for your own situation and type of action.

1. **COORDINATION:** You need a small team to coordinate and lead the effort. This team will make sure that everything fits together, responsibilities are carried out, meetings called, and decisions communicated. This might be the same people who have facilitated your group so far, perhaps with some new people added.

2. **RECRUITMENT:** Everyone in your group should recruit at every opportunity, but the recruitment team takes special responsibility. They work to draw in allies and supporters for demonstrations and needed tasks. They use means like setting up phone trees, developing e-mail lists, sending out mailings, circulating sign-up sheets at meetings and actions, leafleting on college campuses, etc. They create a brief, attractive flyer to invite people to the action, possibly with a map indicating the precise site of the demonstration. Keep three lists of people with names, phones, and e-mail addresses: (1) Regular attenders at your meetings; (2) Those who come to demonstrations; (3) Potential supporters to draw in. If recruiters talk to people who can't come to a meeting or action, they ask them if they could do something else, such as writing a letter to the editor.

3. **PRESS:** Relating to the media is a vital function, since the mass media can be a primary way of getting out your message as well as involving people in the campaign. If someone in the action group has media experience—or if you can recruit someone—their talents are invaluable. If such a person is not available, find someone who is willing to learn how to do media relations. Some key tasks are: ➤ appoint a press spokesperson; ➤ develop a press contacts list (news outlets, reporters, editors, producers); ➤ write and distribute press releases; ➤ set up press conferences; ➤ conduct radio/TV interviews; ➤ arrange coverage by columnists; ➤ find "news pegs"(what your group is doing that gives it news value).

4. **SIGNS AND BANNERS:** At the actual demonstration, your main method of communicating with passersby—aside from speeches and person-to-person conversations—will be through signs, banners, and leaflets. There's a real knack to making signs and banners that communicate effectively. Messages must be short, clear, and in large print—you want people hurrying by to be able to read them. Black lettering on a white background is the most readable.

5. **LEAFLETS:** A good leaflet tells the truth simply, briefly, and clearly so as to evoke a positive response in the reader. Guidelines: ➤ One page; ➤ Neat; ➤ Graphically attractive; ➤ Uncluttered; ➤ Accurate; ➤ No jargon; ➤ Big, bold, short title at the top (such as "Should The Church Be Accountable?" or "Why Catholic Women Are Angry."); ➤ Includes how to contact your group for more information or to get involved. *(Note:* Did you forget your press handout? Give the leaflet to reporters.)

6. **POLICE LIAISON:** The police need to be contacted prior to the demonstration to let them know of your purpose, when and where the demonstration will take place, the nonviolent spirit of your action, and to find out if any permit is needed. (You are informing them about what you intend to do, not asking their permission. Be polite, but firm.) The reason for this pre-demonstration contact is nonviolent openness and truthfulness. A practical reason is that actions which surprise the police make them very nervous. They are less likely to act arbitrarily if they know your plans.

7. **LEGAL:** Having one or more attorneys available is especially important if you anticipate arrests. However, they also can help as consultants on the legal aspects of demonstrations (e.g., do you need a permit?) and as observers at the time of an action.

8. **COMMUNICATIONS:** This team acquires and sets up needed communication equipment, such as a sound system or bullhorns for speakers, walkie-talkies, or cell-phone hookups, and a platform if needed.

9. **FINANCES:** This group keeps accurate books, handles banking, pays bills, makes financial reports, develops the budget, and does fundraising. (This latter could include selling literature, bumper stickers, and buttons; hosting a rummage sale; passing a basket at events, mailing fund appeals to potential contributors; and making sure members contribute their fair share).

10. **MONITORS:** Often called peacekeepers or marshals, these people monitor the nonviolent tone of the action, hand out the "Covenant of Nonviolence," answer questions, and intervene nonviolently if there are any disturbances. It's preferable that monitors have special nonviolence training so they can be cool and effective when faced with tasks like handling hecklers. (Many local and national peace groups offer such training, which we discuss in the next section.)

11. **FAMILY SUPPORT AND CHILDCARE:** Offering childcare can help parents participate. Find ways to support family members who are doing important—though less dramatic—jobs back home. Don't let them feel left out and resentful. Affirm that the work they do is as essential as the direct action. If possible, try to switch roles the next time around.

12. **OTHER POSSIBLE TASKS:** ➤ Medical (hot weather? heatstroke?); ➤ Scout demonstration site or route ahead of time; ➤ Photography; ➤ Special equipment (speakers' podium? stage for street theater?); ➤ Transportation coordination; ➤ Singers and song sheets; ➤ Nonviolent chants; ➤ Water; ➤ Food; ➤ Clean-up.

# Train for Direct Action

## WHY NONVIOLENCE TRAINING?

In the early 1960s, James Orange was a member of a tough street gang in Birmingham, Alabama. When Dr. Martin Luther King's organization came to town to organize anti-segregation marches, Jim decided to participate. Marching down the street, he responded instinctively when a White segregationist hit a woman marcher—he punched the man back. As he tells the story, "The march's marshals surrounded me, took me back to the church, and 'workshopped' me." They role-played the punching scene over and over until Jim found a courageous but nonviolent way to respond to violent attacks. He learned to "let his anger drive his intelligence," to turn his anger into effective loving action. As a result Jim became one of King's best field organizers, orchestrating large nonviolent demonstrations in cities both North and South.

Even though there are Catholic groups that strongly resist reform, it seems highly unlikely they will use the kind of violence that pummeled the civil rights movement. However, it's always wise to be prepared—who knows if some overzealous person will strike out? Nonviolence training helps demonstrators think through creative solutions to conflict. It also helps them develop the confidence to act calmly and with good-will in tense situations. In addition, it helps participants get a realistic feel for the contemplated action, whether or not conflict occurs.

Arun Gandhi, grandson of Mahatma Gandhi, provides nonviolent training to a group in St. Louis.
*Photo by Ellen Osborne*

There are nonviolence training networks all around the country. Their representatives are skilled trainers in the disciplines and practices of nonviolence. One of the most extensive networks is that of the national Fellowship of Reconciliation (*www.forusa.org*). Also, much material is available on the Internet, especially from the Franciscan-founded Pace e Bene Nonviolence Service (*www.paceebene.org/pace*) and the Philadelphia-based Training for Change (*www.trainingforchange.org*). The website for Training for Change describes the exercises below and many more as well.

## ROLE-PLAY DEMONSTRATION SCENARIOS

We have noted already the usefulness of role-plays when preparing for negotiation sessions. In preparation for a demonstration, role-plays ask people to simulate a situation they think they may encounter, such as hecklers interrupting a speech. Those being trained act out the specific roles involved—the demonstrators, the hecklers, police, onlookers, etc.—with the rest of the group acting as observers. At the end, all the players tell what it was like to be the person they portrayed and consider how the demonstrators could have gotten through to the opposition more effectively.

Even if hostility is not expected, a role-play can help people think through what they need to do to prepare for the action and how they should position themselves when the demonstration happens. "Let's see, I didn't realize it before, but if we stand there, no one will be able to see or hear us."

## QUICK DECISION-MAKING

For this training, the larger group breaks up into smaller groups of four to six people. The facilitator (who can be anyone in the larger group) gives them a hypothetical problem— "Someone faints during your vigil at the cathedral;" "It's starting to rain hard and no one brought a raincoat;" "The police say we can't demonstrate where we planned;" "Someone from Opus Dei is shouting that we're all heretics!" In each situation, the groups are given just a minute to consult together and come up with what they would do. They report to the larger group, and the facilitator writes their ideas on newsprint. Then everyone evaluates and seeks the best solution.

A Voice of the Faithful meeting in Wellesley, Mass. See www.voiceofthefaithful.org.
*Globe Staff Photo*

It's amazing how productive these discussions can be and what they suggest about needed preparations on action day. The exercise also gives groups practice in quick decision-making that simulates the real time pressure often found in demonstrations.

## PARALLEL LINES

This exercise requires at least six to ten people, but can easily involve fifty or more. The facilitator starts by having participants stand in two parallel lines facing each other. Each participant should have a partner. Have everyone reach across the gap to make sure they each have one. (If there's an odd person out, you can ask that person to be an observer.)

Explain that you're going to give each line a role. They are going to have an opportunity to experiment with situations in which a nonviolent response is desired. Although it's natural for participants to giggle and be a little nervous, remind them that the more seriously they take this, the more they will learn.

**LINE A**

● ● ● ● ● ● ● ● ● ● ●

● **FACILITATOR**

● ● ● ● ● ● ● ● ● ● ●

**LINE B**

The facilitator gives separate instructions to each line, such as: "Line A, each one of you is a demonstrator with your Church reform group, standing in front of the Catholic cathedral in your hometown. You are there to question the diocese's decision to close financially viable but poor inner-city parishes while providing large loans to a suburban Church that wants to build a carillon." "Line B, each of you is a member of Faithful Voice (a group formed in opposition to Voice of the Faithful). You are outraged that these people would have the effrontery to question the bishop's decision. You want to do everything you can to talk them out of (or, if necessary, knock them out of) this disobedience to established authority."

Tell the groups they can play their roles any way they want. "Think about not only what you're going to say, but the feelings you want to express and the body language you'll use to express them." Give the participants about thirty seconds to get into their roles. Then give the signal to begin.

While the play is going on, the facilitator is going to observe how each side behaves, especially whether Line A is able to stay in a nonviolent spirit and demeanor. Are they able to get their message across to their opponents? Watch for body language as well as what's said. Clenched fists? Arms not crossed, but open at the sides? Eye contact or not? Call out "Cut!" when it seems people are running out of ideas.

Ask people first to express what they felt during the action. Then ask the participants in Line B whether their partners did or said anything that got through to them. Have people discuss what they learned. "Do we need to prepare better or modify our plans in response to what we've just been through?"

## Step 10:
# Make a Final Appeal

### WHY A FINAL APPEAL?

You're now just a step away from direct action. Both Gandhi and King felt it important to give the power-holders every opportunity to correct the injustice or wrong on which attention has been focused. This was based on their belief in the sacred humanity of all, even their most adamant opponents. Everyone has the capacity to do what is right; to act out of conscience instead of self-interest. They should be given every reasonable opportunity to exercise that capacity. By making a final appeal before taking direct action, we offer those in power the opportunity to make things right.

Another reason for a final appeal has to do with the dynamics of nonviolence itself. Part of the power of nonviolent action is that it builds momentum. A well-publicized final appeal can focus public attention more clearly on the issue and elicit energy for change in the wider community.

### HOW TO MAKE THE APPEAL

The best form for your appeal will depend on the unique circumstances surrounding your campaign. One effective means is to write an open letter to the power-holders, reminding them of all that has happened so far, the reasonableness and justice of your proposals for change, the many times that you have appealed to them, and the intransigence of their response. You feel you have no alternative but to start a campaign of direct-action demonstrations to bring your proposals to them more forcefully. But you want to give them one more opportunity to do what is right, so you will wait for two weeks (or whatever) in hopes of a positive response. If you have not heard by then, you will initiate demonstrations.

Gandhi

Such a letter should be well publicized so as many people as possible will be aware of your plans. Certainly, you will want to send copies to all your mailing and e-mail lists, especially people who've been involved in planning and training for the direct action. This may be an excellent time to hold a press conference to release the letter, explain to the media why you are taking this step, and answer their questions. The open letter, or a statement based on it, could also be sent to newspapers as an op-ed piece, or if you have the funds, run as a paid advertisement. Your group will likely be aware of many venues through which you can send your appeal.

A wonderful model of such an appeal is Dr. Martin Luther King's "Letter from a Birmingham Jail," available on the Internet and in many books about Dr. King. This appeal came in the midst of a campaign rather than at the beginning, but it has all the elements that make such an appeal powerful.

One more thought: Crucial to the power of both Gandhi and King's nonviolent movements was their rooting in religious community. Gandhi held regular prayer meetings, attended by thousands. These gatherings not only sought God's help and guidance, but also provided time for planning, announcements, and other movement business. Dr. King's movement was based almost entirely in the Black church, with its powerful sermons, inspiring gospel music, shared suffering, and deep sense of community. What about holding the press conference on the steps of a church at the close of a worship service you've organized to pray for God's love and guidance throughout the upcoming demonstration days?

**Loaves and Fishes**                                                    *Julie Lonemann*

# Step 11:
# Take Loving Direct Action

By this time, your group will have chosen the final decision-makers on whom the direct action is focused, your goals and overall strategy, and the method or methods you will use. Since most direct action involves some kind of public demonstrations, here are some specific suggestions for organizing demonstrations.

To keep us aware of Jesus walking with us, all the groups that gather to handle the tasks below should provide time in and around their meetings for prayer, worship, singing, and anything else that makes us aware of the Spirit's guidance. This will provide composure and give a sense of joining with God, "who practices kindness, justice and righteousness in the earth" (Jer. 9:24). A quick way of praying: Have group members stand in a circle, arms over one another's shoulders, eyes closed. Ask anyone who feels moved to say a prayer.

## A FEW DAYS BEFORE THE DEMONSTRATION

1. **PRESS TEAM:** Contact all media—sending out releases, doing interviews, answering questions. Make sure a press spokesperson has been chosen to talk to the media during the demonstrations, especially on the first day. Assign someone to make reminder calls to media persons early on action day. (Most press coverage for that day is assigned by 8:30 AM.). If the outlet can't send a reporter, see if you can arrange to call and do an interview from the demonstration site.

March on Washington, 1963

2. **SIGNS, BANNERS, AND LEAFLETS:** Pick people to take these to the demonstration site. Someone should be in charge of getting people to carry the banners and signs; another person should find volunteers to hand out the leaflets. One of the leaflets should be the "Covenant of Nonviolence."

3. **POLICE LIAISON:** Reiterate your nonviolent commitment and give the police a general outline of your plans. It's not necessary to tell the police *all* your plans, as some kinds of demonstrations have confidential elements. However, in general, openness with police is the best policy. Lack of openness can easily lead to mistrust and even spying by police intelligence units who want to be sure they have the information they feel they need. If you are open and nonviolent, you contribute to one of the few valuable forms of unemployment in the country—fewer jobs for spies, infiltrators, and agents provocateurs.

4. **TRAINING:** Be sure to have a final training for participants. In large actions, trainers may need to secure a large building such as a church where people can be trained as monitors or to fill other roles.

5. **COORDINATION:** Meet to make final plans (including contingency plans), to make sure all the necessary responsibilities are assigned, and to make any needed decisions on rendezvous points and the timing.

## ON DEMONSTRATION DAY

1. **PRESS TEAM:** Make the early morning calls to media outlets. At TV stations, try to talk with the assignment editor—she or he tells reporters what stories to cover. Do you have a press spokesperson? Press releases?

2. **COORDINATORS:** Do your best to be relaxed, calm, and friendly. Don't run around, shout orders, or act self-important. You have a leadership role—but as a servant-leader. Since some participants will have just heard of the action and are joining the group for the first time, coordinators need to bring them up to date.

3. **KICKOFF:** Well before the action is to begin, get all the demonstration participants together to go over last-minute details and motivate people. Here is an example of a coordinator's remarks, based on our illustration:

> **Welcome:** It's great to see so many of you here. My name is _____ and I'm one of the coordinators today. First, I'd like to celebrate everyone who has made the commitment to participate in today's action. (If participants do not all know each other, invite people to raise hands if they're, for example, on the Coordinating Team, from an urban parish, from a suburban parish, over seventy years old, under fifteen years old, etc.)

> **Why we are here:** Our overall goal is to have our bishop move from his grandiose mansion to a residence more in keeping with his commitments as a follower of Christ. Our goal today is simply to get our bishop to meet with us. We have tried for months to arrange such a meeting so we can work together to build a better Church. We are faithful Catholics who love our Church. But, time and again, our bishop has refused to meet with us. Today, we are here to demonstrate that we are serious.

> **"Covenant of nonviolence:"** Our action today is based on gospel nonviolence. We want to express to all the kind of love Jesus

*LOVE IN ACTION*

showed, even to those who opposed him. Be sure to take a copy of the covenant and read it carefully. If there is anyone here today who feels they cannot abide by the covenant, we ask them not to join our demonstration.

**What we will do today:** In a few minutes, we will go together to the bishop's mansion, carrying our banner asking, "Where Would Jesus Live?" Monitors will help keep us orderly and will handle any disruptions from the outside that may occur. Leafleters will accompany us. Please refer any inquiries from the press to our Press Team. Carry signs and banners so they are visible to passers-by. When our demonstration ends at (specify time), you are invited to stay for a brief evaluation of what we did well, how we could improve, and our next steps.

**Pray:** Let's begin with prayer. As we continue through the day, let's keep praying as individuals, asking especially that our bishop be open to us, and that we act like disciples of Jesus.

4. **POINTERS ON PROCESSIONS:** A well-organized march to the site can add drama and forcefulness to a demonstration. If you plan to do one, the following points are important to remember:

**LEADERSHIP:** Coordinators or other informed people (folks who know the route of march) should be at the front of the line. Walk slowly, so people at the end don't have to run to keep up. Monitors should walk calmly alongside the line.

**SPACING:** Don't bunch up. You want passersby to see your signs and banners. Monitors should encourage people to space themselves with a yard or so between them.

**Procession**                                                    Julie Lonemann

**TONE:** A silent, prayerful march or one where everyone is singing is much more impressive than one in which participants are gabbing informally among themselves.

**COMMUNICATION:** A bullhorn is helpful for communication with the group. Monitors acting as "runners" or using cell phones can help the front of the line keep in touch with the rest.

**SINGING:** If you have music, be sure the amplification system is at the very front (pointed back toward the line) or the very rear (pointed front) so everyone can hear and sing together.

## AT THE DEMONSTRATION SITE

**PRESS TEAM:** Looks for reporters, gets their names and affiliations, gives them the press release and/or flyer, answers questions, directs them to spokespersons for interviews, calls to do phone interviews with media who expressed interest but haven't shown up. (There's nothing like a hot interview from the scene of a good action.) Be sure to bring cell phones for such contacts.

**COORDINATORS:** See that the demonstrators position themselves effectively and that signs and banners can easily be read by passersby and motorists. Don't let people block public throughways. (In most locales, demonstrators can be on the sidewalk as long as they don't block it.) Move around and let people know what's happening. If it's a long demonstration, set up rest periods, rotate breaks, point out public toilets, and provide water and snacks.

**LEAFLETERS:** Station themselves at locations with maximum foot traffic (such as busy corners). Pass out leaflets with a smile, a friendly attitude, and a comment like, "This explains what those demonstrators over there are doing." Make sure every demonstrator (including any new people who join) get the "Covenant of Nonviolence."

**MONITORS:** Help with effective sign placement, deal nonviolently with any troublemakers or hecklers. Act as servants to the group—friendly, warm, and helpful, rather than strutting or bossy.

**POLICE LIAISON:** Introduce themselves to any police officers who are present and explain the action's purpose and nonviolent commitment. Share the leaflet and Covenant. Let police know you're available to answer questions. Remember that sometimes higher-ups put pressure on police to try to prevent an action or limit its effectiveness (such as by saying you can't demonstrate where you planned). Many a demonstration would not have happened if demonstrators immediately obeyed police who said, "You can't do that." Be friendly and willing to negotiate nonessentials, but be clear and firm about your goals, legal rights, what you intend to do, and why. Freedom of speech and assembly, and petitioning for redress of grievances are basic constitutional rights.

If police are not flexible and say they will make arrests, you can move to another spot. If some members are committed to civil disobedience and have thought through the implications, then they can stay at the site while others move a little bit away and act as observers.

**RECRUITMENT TEAM:** Get names, phone numbers, mail, and e-mail addresses of new people who express interest. Invite them to the next demonstration or group meeting.

## IF DISRUPTION OCCURS

Probably you will not face aggressive verbal or physical opposition. If you do, remember what you learned in nonviolence training. Take a deep breath, center yourself, and pray. These opponents are misguided, but they are still beloved children of God. Treat them with *agape* love.

In the unlikely event that you are physically attacked, stay calm, centered, and prayerful. Don't run or shout. Don't break ranks except to help someone who is hurt. Keep your hands at your sides or open in front of you. Make clear you have no weapons and no intention of hitting back. Try to show goodwill, to "overcome evil with good" (Rom. 12:21). Be creative and try to take nonviolent initiative. "Brother/sister, I'm a Christian—and I'm going to try to keep loving you, no matter what you do."

As a group, start singing or saying a prayer together. Hold hands and kneel. If violence escalates, meet it with escalating love.

## TO END THE ACTION

At the agreed time, call people together.

  ✠ Thank participants for coming.
  ✠ Announce any upcoming meetings and activities.
  ✠ What did you like? What would you like to see next time?
  ✠ Close with prayer.

This faith-based demonstration against the war in Iraq took months of careful planning.
*Photo by Ryan Rodrick Beiler, courtesy of www.sojo.net*

# Step 12:
# Celebrate, Evaluate, Plan Next Steps

## CELEBRATE

Even if you haven't achieved all your goals and objectives, be sure to celebrate what you *have* accomplished at your next meeting. Of course, if you've been in a campaign that has accomplished its goals, it's time for a big celebration. Do something really enjoyable. Hold a big potluck. Put together a concert with the songs you've sung and time for people to say what the campaign has meant to them.

If you've truly had success, don't rush right into the next campaign. Gandhi's campaigns and the civil rights movement had a rhythm of intense actions followed by time to recuperate. In the civil rights movement, they called it "laying in the cut." Catch up on the sleep you've been missing. Do some things that renew you. Chill.

## EVALUATE

Most campaigns will require a series of actions before anything that can be called "success" is achieved. Take time between specific actions, therefore, to evaluate:

**Positives?** What have we done really well so far? What's working? What's been most enjoyable?

**Do better?** What are some areas where we can improve? How?

## PLAN NEXT STEPS

Assuming your campaign is ongoing, plan carefully what you'll do next. Some things to ask:

- ✚ Are our assumptions holding up, or do we need to change or add to them?
- ✚ Is our strategy still valid in light of how the campaign has developed?
- ✚ Are our tactics working?
- ✚ What have we learned about the gatekeepers and power-holders? How do we need to revise our strategic estimate in light of this?
- ✚ Do we need to do more to deepen our group's nonviolent commitment? Do we need to firm up our organizational structure?

Answering these questions will help you decide how to make the next action have its greatest effect.

# NOTES

1. Here are two books giving dozens of examples of ordinary people carrying out nonviolent campaigns: Peter Ackerman and Jack Duvall, *A Force More Powerful: A Century of Nonviolent Conflict* (New York: Saint Martin's Press, 2000); Gene Sharp, *The Politics of Nonviolent Action* (Boston: Porter Sargent, 1973).

2. Martin Luther King Jr. lists six steps in his book, *Stride Toward Freedom* (New York: Harper and Row, 1958), but they cover almost exactly the same points as our twelve steps.

3. John Dear, *Disarming the Heart* (New York: Paulist, 1987), 121.

4. Monica Brown, *Embodying the God We Proclaim: Ministering as Jesus Did* (San Jose: Resource Publications, Inc., 1997), 16.

5. Mary Lou Kownacki, *Love Beyond Measure: A Spirituality of Nonviolence* (Erie: Pax Christi USA, 1993), 2.

6. "Anger, whether expressed by Jesus or directed at him, was always from or about a single issue: the abuse of power by the religious leaders of his day or their failure to respect the believers." Remarks by Fr. Thomas Doyle at the Voice of the Faithful's "Priests of Integrity" award, Worcester, Mass., November 13, 2004. For examples of Jesus' anger toward religious leaders, see Matt. 15:1–9; 22:18; 23:23–31; Mark 3:1–6; Luke 12:56; 13:10–17.

7. Sharon Browning, "Of Love and Activism." Scripture reflection at St. Vincent de Paul Church,  Philadelphia, Pa.

8. Martin Luther King Jr., "Nonviolence and Racial Justice," *Christian Century,* Feb. 6, 1957, 166.

9. Ibid.

10. Martin Luther King Jr., *Strength to Love* (New York: Pocket Books, 1964),  44.

11. Martin Luther King, "Nonviolence and Racial Justice," *Christian Century,* 166. See also King, *Strength to Love,* Chapter 5, "Loving Your Enemies," 41–50.

12. John L. Alien, Jr., *All the Pope's Men: The Inside Story of How the Vatican Really Thinks* (New York: Doubleday, 2004), 93.

13. Stephen B. Dates, *Let the Trumpet Sound: The Life of Martin Luther King Jr.* (New York: Harper, 1982), 211.

14. Gene Sharp, *Waging Nonviolent Struggle: 20th Century Practice and 21st Century Potential* (Boston: Porter Sargent, 2005), 448. Much has been written in the last thirty years about strategic planning. It is used by businesses, the military, citizens' organizations, political candidates, and many others. If you are interested in learning more about strategic planning, do a library or Internet search.

15. If you have done strategic planning in the past, you know there are several schools of such planning and, therefore, several ways to state

its elements. A different breakdown than ours, for example, states its elements as: Mission > Assumptions > Goals > Objectives > Strategies > Tactics > Tasks. Another approach simply uses Assumptions > Goals > Strategies > Tactics. Each is a way to do disciplined planning. Each approach begins with the broad view—Vision, Mission, Purpose—and ends with highly specific tasks. Always, the underlying questions are "What do we want to do? How are we going to do it?" It is a way for organizations or movements to continuously plan for the future by clearly articulating their assumptions, goals and methods and bringing them under constant review. The approach we have chosen in this chapter seems to fit best with the kind of faith-based campaigns we envision.

16. *America,* "News Briefs," May 17, 2004, 5. The Pope gave the speech on April 20, 2004.

17. This description of "One-on-Ones" is taken from workshop notes prepared by Voice of the Faithful (VOTF) staff person, Aimee Carevich Hariramani for a "Many Hands, Many Hearts" workshop, Oct. 30, 2004.

# The Many Methods of Active Nonviolence

Over thirty years ago, Dr. Gene Sharp, working under the auspices of Harvard University's Center for International Affairs, wrote the book, *The Politics of Nonviolent Action*. In it, he made a compendium of 198 different methods of nonviolent direct action—a comprehensive catalogue which never has been surpassed.[1] Though it has been adjusted and refined over the past three decades, Dr. Sharp's classification still stands as the best and most complete catalog of nonviolent tools ever written. We will draw upon it extensively.

A lone Chinese citizen blocking a line of tanks became a symbol of nonviolent courage during China's 1989 Tiananmen Square uprising.

Dr. Sharp points out, however, that we should not limit ourselves to just 198 approaches. "The list is far from complete," he writes. "Many additional methods doubtless exist, and many new ones could certainly be invented."[2] Sharp's list simply suggests the wide range of stratagems available to direct-action groups.

This chapter draws heavily from Dr. Sharp's work, and its list of approaches follow his classifications in most respects. I've selected eighty of his almost-two hundred methods, choosing those most applicable to Church reform and providing a multitude of historical examples of how they have been used from ancient times to the present. I've also included dozens of suggestions for how they might be used for Church reform in contemporary settings.

Since footnoting every reference to *The Politics of Nonviolent Action* would consume a great deal of space, the reader should be aware that, unless otherwise noted, the quotations in the text below appear in Dr. Sharp's book between pages 109 and 445.

## VARIETY OF CREATIVE METHODS FOR CHURCH REFORM

If asked to name all the forms nonviolent action can take, most people would be hard pressed to identify more than a few, such as picketing, marching, sit-ins, and prayer vigils. The nonviolent "toolkit," however, is bulging with a wide variety of potentially applicable tools. Catholics using active nonviolence for Church reform, therefore, can greatly expand their repertoire of possible methods, choosing those most appropriate for their specific campaign.

Students holding a sit-in at a lunch counter in Greensboro, N.C., 1960
*UPI/Bettmann/Corbis*

Whether or not a particular method is used, it is inspiring just to read the illustrative examples and to realize that ordinary people—in every culture and historical period—have used nonviolent direct action courageously and often successfully in their struggles to bring about positive social change.

When planning a nonviolent campaign, organizers may simply run through the list of nonviolent methods asking themselves which might work best to achieve their objectives in their unique situation. The key question is, "Will this tactic put a spotlight on what's wrong and stir people to action?" It may be that one approach will leap out as perfect for a particular campaign. Sometimes one or two methods, used persistently over time, can can bring enormous change. (Remember the huge impact of the lunch counter sit-ins and freedom rides in the segregated U.S. South.)

Usually it is best, however, not to limit oneself to a single tool. Most often, several methods used together simultaneously—or one after another in a series of varied actions—can have the greatest effect. The trick is to weave them together into a comprehensive campaign in which different steps complement each other to strengthen the overall movement for change.

To achieve maximum potential, the tools should fit the group's overall campaign strategy, discussed in Chapter 3, Step 5. It is advisable to plan strategy carefully before choosing a specific method or set of methods. Each direct-action group should pick the tool or tools that show the greatest potential for helping the campaign reach its goals.

Of course, it may be that none of the methods listed here are really appropriate in a particular situation. In that case, your group may need to invent a new direct-action tactic more suitable to your reality. Maybe your new method will become method number 199! Or it may be that some approach other than nonviolent direct action (such as a lawsuit) needs to be considered.

Whatever means are chosen, remember that they can only be considered in accord with gospel nonviolence if they are carried out in a prayerful spirit that shows goodwill toward any opponents. Lacking prayer and goodwill, any means can become just a way of pressuring others to submit, without any redemptive aspect. Without *agape*, these methods can result in inconsequential, or even destructive, actions.

## HOW NONVIOLENT DIRECT ACTION BRINGS ABOUT SOCIAL CHANGE

In addition to categorizing methods, Dr. Sharp's *Politics of Nonviolent Action* also explores how nonviolent direct action brings about change in social, economic, political, and (by implication) religious structures. Dr. Sharp, a political scientist, points out that, although the change-resisting leaders of these structures appear to be very powerful, their power ultimately rests on the consent, cooperation, submission, or support of those who are led. To the degree that nonviolent activists can convince others to withdraw their support, the power and authority of those in leadership are thereby eroded. If such erosion is (or appears to be) severe, if the non-cooperators refuse to be intimidated by negative sanctions from the power-holders, and if the resisters offer a meaningful alternative to the existing structure, then a shift in power can occur, and new possibilities for restructuring can emerge.

**When successful, nonviolent action produces change through the following mechanisms:**

- **Conversion:** Those who have been resisting change "see the light"—they come to agree with what the actionists are advocating. Ultimately, they come to *want* to make the proposed changes.

- **Accommodation:** The power-holders do not agree with the proposed changes, but nevertheless conclude it is best to grant some or all of the actionists' demands. Often this is because power-holders realize they will lose more by continuing their opposition than by conceding gracefully.

- **Necessitation:** The power-holders do not change their minds. They want to hold onto the status quo, but are unable to do so. The sources of their power and means of control have been reduced or taken away. People who had been submissive now refuse obedience. The power-holders are forced to give in.

- **Disintegration:** The former leaders' sources of power are so completely severed or dissolved that the structure they are defending simply falls apart as a viable entity, making room for new structures and a new approach.

Dr. Sharp builds on this understanding of the dynamics of nonviolent social change in an article in *The Ecumenical Review*:[3]

Nonviolent action is a technique for mobilizing and applying the power potential of people and groups for pursuing objectives and interests by nonmilitary "weapons"—psychological, political, social, economic, and spiritual . . . People using this technique either refuse to do things they are expected or required to do, or they insist on doing things they normally do not do or which are forbidden . . . Faced with such a challenge to their very sources of power, opponents can be expected to apply repression. This repression, however, is often ineffective in halting the nonviolent struggle and can alienate various groups, so that the repression actually weakens the opponents and strengthens the nonviolent struggle group.[4]

Christian demonstrators celebrate Pentecost by calling for effective anti-poverty programs.
*Photo by Ryan Rodrick Beiler, courtesy of www.sojo.net*

Dr. Sharp's analysis has special sting and poignancy for those of us involved in Church reform. His analysis—applied to the Church—would assume that unsympathetic priests and bishops are able to be secretive, dismissive, abusive, and all the other things for which we criticize them only *because the rest of us allow them to act in this way*. We do not, at a deep level, challenge them to be something different. We do not withdraw our consent, cooperation, submission, or support.

Do we behave submissively, perhaps, because we do not want to pay the price of Christian adulthood? Do we find it easier to be led than to take our own responsibility? Or do we fear the sanctions those in charge can impose, such as criticism, shutting down parishes, excommunication? Or is it because we don't see how to challenge effectively the negative features of clerical culture?

What follows are a host of creative, empowering methods, illuminated by powerful historical examples and inventive suggestions for contemporary application. My hope is that these will move us beyond impotence, passivity, complaint, or withdrawal into effective nonviolent action to reform and renew our beloved Church.

# Summary List: 80 Nonviolent Methods

## I. ACTIONS TO SEND A MESSAGE
### Nonviolent Protest and Persuasion

**FORMAL STATEMENTS**
1. Public Speeches
2. Letters of Opposition or Support
3. Declarations by Individuals and Organizations
4. Signed Public Statements
5. Group or Mass Petitions

**COMMUNICATION WITH A WIDER AUDIENCE**
6. Slogans, Satire, Caricatures, and Symbols
7. Banners, Posters, Bumper Stickers, and Displays
8. Leaflets, Flyers, Pamphlets, Articles, and Books
9. Newspapers and Journals
10. Radio, TV, Press Conferences, CDs, Cell Phones, and the Internet
11. Skywriting and Earth-Writing

**GROUP REPRESENTATIONS**
12. Deputations
13. Mock Awards
14. Group Lobbying
15. Picketing
16. Mock Elections

**SYMBOLIC PUBLIC ACTS**
17. Displays of Flags and Symbolic Colors
18. Wearing of Symbols
19. Photos
20. Prayer and Worship
21. Delivering Symbolic Objects
22. Symbolic Lights
23. Symbolic Sounds

**PRESSURE ON INDIVIDUALS**
24. "Haunting" or "Shadowing"
25. Fraternization
26. Vigils

**DRAMA AND MUSIC**
27. Humorous Skits, Street Theater, and Pranks
28. Performances of Plays and Music
29. Singing
30. Films

**PROCESSIONS**

31. Marches
32. Parades
33. Religious Processions
34. Pilgrimages
35. Motorcades

**HONORING THE DEAD**

36. Mourning
37. Mock Funerals
38. Homage at Burial Places

**PUBLIC ASSEMBLIES**

39. Assemblies of Protest or Support
40. Teach-Ins

**WITHDRAWAL AND RENUNCIATION**

41. Walk-Outs
42. Silence
43. Renouncing Honors
44. Turning One's Back

# II. ACTIONS TO SUSPEND COOPERATION AND ASSISTANCE

## Social Noncooperation

**OSTRACISM OF PERSONS**

45. Social Boycott
46. Selective Social Boycott

**NONCOOPERATION WITH SOCIAL EVENTS, CUSTOMS, AND INSTITUTIONS**

47. Suspension of Social and Sports Activities
48. Boycott of Social Affairs
49. Student Strike
50. Social Disobedience
51. Withdrawal from Social Institutions
52. Nonobedience and Disguised Disobedience

**WITHDRAWAL FROM THE SOCIAL SYSTEM**

53. Stay-at-Home
54. Sanctuary

## Economic Noncooperation

**ACTION BY CONSUMERS**

55. Consumer Boycott
56. Policy of Austerity

Street speaking in front of painted panels representing impact of U.S. military aid to Pakistan.

# Description of Nonviolent Methods

The classifications below are divided into three broad categories: (1) protest and persuasion, (2) noncooperation, and (3) nonviolent intervention. Within each category is a list of specific methods, eighty in all. Each entry begins with a brief description of the method, then offers one or more examples of how this tool has been used by in the past (HISTORICAL) and in the present (CONTEMPORARY). If appropriate, we also will provide a brief scenario of how this particular line of action might be used now as part of a nonviolent campaign for CHURCH REFORM. Only those methods most pertinent to Church reform and renewal are included.

### Which method?

How does one know which method to choose at any given time? Actions in the first category are more based on persuasion, reaching people's consciences, and educating the public. Therefore, they may be most appropriate for the early stages of a campaign. Methods of noncooperation (2) and intervention (3)— which escalate the pressure on power-holders—might be reserved for later in the campaign if purely persuasive methods have not brought desired results.

### About the term *Opponents*

We sometimes use the word opponent. This usage reflects the reality that people committed to nonviolent social change inevitably will run into opposition. From the point of view of gospel nonviolence, however, "opponents" are human beings, made in the image of God. Like us, they can change. We are trying to win them over, not defeat them. Maybe they have a piece of the truth that we need. We always are open to negotiations to try to reach a settlement. We are committed to treating them at all times with reconciling goodwill and *agape* love.

### Remember the Importance of Media Coverage

The impact of these methods can be greatly enhanced by media coverage. If a group or individual takes action without informing the press, only people in the immediate vicinity will see and hear it. However, if the action is covered on television, radio, the newspapers, and the Internet, a much wider audience, possibly in the hundreds of thousands or even millions, can become better informed about the issue. Perhaps others will be moved to take similar action.

# I. ACTIONS TO SEND A MESSAGE
## NONVIOLENT PROTEST AND PERSUASION

*This category includes a large number of methods that are mainly symbolic acts of peaceful opposition or attempted persuasion.[5] Using them may simply show that protestors are against something (such as parishioners protesting a pastor's refusal to convene meetings of the parish finance council), or in favor of something (like a proposal that laity be included in an important Church decision-making body). This class of nonviolent actions often expresses deep personal feelings or moral condemnation of a policy or statement (such as to persuade diocesan officials not to close a poor but viable inner-city parish.)*

## Formal Statements

### 1. PUBLIC SPEECHES, MEETINGS, AND CONFERENCES

*Verbal statements to a public audience for or against some issue, policy, system, or condition (including sermons in a church, formal addresses to a public gathering, or spontaneous speeches to a crowd gathered for action).*

HISTORICAL: **Norway, April 25, 1941:** Thousands of teachers, refusing to comply with Nazi occupation decrees, each read a **public statement** to their students: "Teachers must . . . teach their pupils to believe in and uphold truth and justice. Therefore, teachers cannot, without betraying their calling, teach anything that violates their conscience . . . That, I promise you, I shall not do." When Norway's Nazi-appointed, fascist head of state, Vidkun Quisling, was ordered by Hitler to give up efforts to bend Norway to his will, Quisling grumbled, "You teachers have destroyed everything for me."[6]

Methods of protest and persuasion are typically used early in a campaign. Strategically, they serve to accomplish these things:

**Involve** more people in the initial stages of a campaign.

**Persuade** power-holders by calling attention to an injustice in a way that tries to jog their consciences and convince them to change.

**Signal** to power-holders the depth of feeling around the issue which will likely lead to more intensified action if a change is not made.

**Communicate** with the general public in order to arouse support for the desired change.

**Influence** an aggrieved group so they will take action themselves.

**When employed later in a campaign, protest and persuasion add strength to a campaign by accompanying and complementing acts of noncooperation or nonviolent intervention.**

CONTEMPORARY: **Boston, July 20, 2002:** Fr. Thomas Doyle's **rousing speech** to the inaugural meeting of Voice of the Faithful (VOTF) inspired many attenders to return to their hometowns and form local VOTF affiliates dedicated to ending sex abuse in the Church. ✠ **Cabrini College, Radnor, Penn., April 23, 2005:** VOTF of Greater Philadelphia invited members of parish-finance councils and held a **conference on "Financial Accountability in the Church,"** with expert speakers and panelists, which raised the question of how Church funds are being spent and why finance councils either have not been set up in parishes or, if they have, are so tightly controlled by the pastor that the laity have little or no voice in them.

CHURCH REFORM: If the U.S. continues its "empire-building" foreign policy, hold a **conference on "Christianity and Empire."** Examine issues like why Church leadership, during President Bush's election campaign, advocated denying the Eucharist to candidates who supported same-sex marriage and abortion but said nothing about politicians supporting our wars and voting money for them. Explore how the Church can be outspoken in its peace teachings. ✠ Many **U.S. bishops** moved sexually abusive priests among parish assignments without warning parents or police. U.S. bishops, aware of widespread abuse, did not take concerted national action to address it until the press broke the story. Psychologically troubled, abusive priests have faced criminal action and Church penalties, but what about these "cover-up bishops"? What about holding a **conference** with experts (canon law, theology, Church history, and criminal law) to explore the U.S. bishops' responsibility for the crisis and whether any consequences—in addition to the bad publicity they've received—should flow from their failures?

## 2. LETTERS OF OPPOSITION OR SUPPORT

*Can be either private or "open" public letters from individuals or groups, original or form letters, signed by one or more people. Gains significance when signed by well-known persons.*

HISTORICAL: **World War II:** Bulgarians sent a flood of **letters and telegrams** to parliament, cabinet members, statesmen, and social and political leaders, objecting to a Nazi-sponsored anti-Jewish law. Part of a movement that saved the entire Bulgarian Jewish population from the death camps.

CONTEMPORARY: **Amnesty International** regularly uses **targeted letter-writing** to press for the freedom of those unjustly jailed.

CHURCH REFORM: Set a goal of sending **one thousand letters** to the Vatican's Congregation for Divine Worship explaining why their insistence on **sexist male language** in liturgical texts is offensive, not only to women, but to all believers in social justice.

## 3. DECLARATIONS BY INDIVIDUALS AND ORGANIZATIONS

*Written statements of such a quality or which produce such a response that the declaration itself becomes influential in shaping people's loyalties and behavior. Endorsement of a statement by prominent organizations can add weight and seriousness to the issue being addressed.*

HISTORICAL: Martin Luther's 95 Theses (1517); The United States Declaration of Independence (1776); The "Freedom Charter" of the

South African antiapartheid movement (1955). ✢ **Netherlands, February 1943:** Dutch Reformed and Roman Catholic Church both issued **pastoral letters** urging congregations not to cooperate with Nazi occupation forces.

CONTEMPORARY: Voice of the Faithful's 2002 **founding statement** became a rallying cry for people around the country to form local affiliates and work toward VOTF's mission and goals. ✢ **Boston, December 13, 2002:** When Cardinal Bernard Law clung to power, despite massive evidence that he had approved transfer of disturbed, abusive priests from one assignment to another, a **statement of concern** by fifty-eight Boston priests forced him to step down.

CHURCH REFORM: Circulate broadly for discussion **the declaration, "Counsel and Consent,"** by the Bridgeport VOTF, which presents a vision for a restructured Church in which the laity have a meaningful voice in its governance (see *www.votfbpt.org*).

## 4. SIGNED PUBLIC STATEMENTS

*A declaration aimed at officials, the general public, an opponent, or all three that is released to the press with the signatures of supporters.*

CONTEMPORARY: Catholic bishops frequently issue **"pastoral letters"** on moral concerns, such as the influential 1983 peace pastoral, "The Challenge of Peace," written by U.S. bishops. ✢ **November, 2001:** Soulforce, an interfaith organization working for the inclusion of gay and lesbian people into the Church, maintains an annual nonviolent presence at the U.S. Conference of Bishops. It began by publishing an **open letter to the bishops on "Natural Law" theology.** See *www.soulforce.org/ article/392*.

CHURCH REFORM: Work with **non-Catholic ordained women clergy** to write a letter to appropriate Catholic officials, reflecting on their call to ordained ministry, their experience as clergy, and their hope that the Catholic Church will change its policy of making gender rather than gifts the criterion for ordination. ✢ Could a group of priests, abuse survivors, and ordinary laity sign a statement urging the bishops to consider a **"restorative justice" approach for abusive priests** as an alternative to the current adversarial approach?

## 5. GROUP OR MASS PETITIONS

*Written to seek redress for a specific grievance, signed by large numbers of people or by individuals acting on behalf of organizations.*

HISTORICAL: In the years **AD 183–185**, members of the village of Aga Bey in Asia Minor **petition Roman Emperor Septimus for relief from city taxes,** since they live in the countryside. They threaten a work stoppage if relief was not granted. It was.

CONTEMPORARY: **June, 2005:** Voice of the Faithful (VOTF) collects signatures for a **petition** to be hand-delivered to Archbishop William Lavada, new Prefect of the Congregation for the Doctrine of the Faith, urging him to keep open the case of accused sex abuser, Fr. Marcial Maciel Degollado, founder of Legionnaires of Christ. Maciel was later relieved of his duties by the Vatican. ✠ **October 2005:** the Catholic reform group **FutureChurch collected thirty-five thousand signatures** on a petition asking for open discussion of mandatory celibacy and women deacons. Executive Director Sr. Chris Shenk delivered the petition to the International Synod on Eucharist in Rome, and subsequently was quoted in the Associated Press, *New York Times*, British Broadcasting Corporation, National Public Radio, Religious News Service, and by Spanish and Swiss television.

CHURCH REFORM: To build support and commitment in the movement, get several thousand Catholics to sign a **petition** to their bishop, asking that complete, audited **diocesan financial reports** be published publicly to allow the faithful to examine them.

## Communication with a Wider Audience

Demanding the vote, 1916

*Both visual and oral, these methods are designed to influence power-holders, seek support from third parties, or gain members or assistance for the nonviolent group.*

### 6. SLOGANS, SATIRE, CARICATURES, AND SYMBOLS

*May be "written, painted, drawn, printed, mimed, gestured, or spoken."*

HISTORICAL: In **1942, Polish resistance to the Nazis** was sustained in part by a group of "mischievous and diabolically clever" youngsters called "The Little Wolves." Going out at night, they used indelible paint to write **slogans** such as "Poland Fights On" on German trucks, autos, houses, and even the backs of Germans themselves. ✠ **Summer and fall 1971:** Direct Action Committee of the Friends of East Bengal painted a 5' x 40' **portable mural** depicting the connection between U.S. military aid to West Pakistan and the mass killings taking place in East Pakistan. Used in street demonstrations and other forms of direct action, this supported Bengali resistance and had a significant role in pressuring Congress to cut off the aid. This helped the nation of Bangladesh come into existence.[7]

### 7. BANNERS, POSTERS, BUMPER STICKERS, AND DISPLAYS

*Frequently used to promote a group's message or challenge those in power.*

HISTORICAL: During President Wilson's address to Congress on **Dec. 4, 1916**, five members of a **woman-suffragist organization** unrolled a yellow sateen **banner from the visitors' gallery** saying, "Mr. President, What Will You Do for Woman Suffrage?" Through these and other actions, women got the vote shortly after World War I.

CONTEMPORARY: In the late 1990s, the Women's Ordination Conference (WOC) purchased **billboard space** across the United States affirming Catholic women's call to the priesthood. ✚ Many direct-action groups put their names, slogans, and symbols on **bumper stickers**.

CHURCH REFORM: Local bishop lives in **palatial mansion**. Reform group attempts to meet with him to discuss moving out. If no progress, they stretch a **banner across the building that asks, "WHERE WOULD JESUS LIVE?"**

## 8. LEAFLETS, FLYERS, PAMPHLETS, ARTICLES, AND BOOKS

*Used to express opposition to power-holder policies and to make a call to resistance, these can become a method of nonviolent action. Leaflets are the most common method, but books are examples as well.*

HISTORICAL: **Books:** Gandhi's autobiography, *The Story of My Experiments with Truth* (1940); Nelson Mandela's *Long Walk to Freedom* (1994); and Martin Luther King's "Letter from a Birmingham Jail" (widely distributed as a booklet) were all influential in promoting nonviolent resistance. Fr. John Courtney Murray's book, *We Hold These Truths*, plus numerous articles in scholarly theological journals, helped reverse the Church's position on democracy and religious freedom during the 1950s and 1960s.[8]

Barbara Blaine at the Vatican, holding photos of herself as a child.
*Image courtesy of www.snapnetwork.org*

CONTEMPORARY: **Rome, April 11, 2005:** Barbara Blaine, president of Survivors Network for those Abused by Priests (SNAP) **leafleted at the Vatican**, protesting hierarchy's decision to allow disgraced Boston Cardinal Bernard Law concelebrate an important Mass during the papal conclave. Interviewed by World Press, Blaine held a photo taken of herself at age 12 in 1969, when a priest began four years of molesting her sexually. ✚ **Summer 1994:** Philadelphia's Cardinal Anthony Bevilacqua began sending to parishes a newsletter titled *The Voice of Your Shepherd*. Immediately after each of the Cardinal's newsletters appeared, an anonymous group calling itself C.O.R.E. (Catholics Organized for Renewal Everywhere) sent out their own **newsletter, *The Sheep Talk Baaaack.*** Challenging the designation of the faithful as "sheep," it pointed out that the dictionary defines *sheep* as "a person who is meek, stupid, timid, defenseless." It urged the Cardinal to choose a more respectful title, saying that "as adult members of the Catholic Church with equal baptismal dignity, we are affronted to have our leader refer to us in this manner." C.O.R.E. applauded the Cardinal's positive initiatives (such as allowing female altar servers), but critiqued steps it judged as harmful to the Church (his support for the ban on women's ordination). ✠ **Long Island, New York, 2005:** VOTF members and clergy sex-abuse survivors stand outside St. Agnes Cathedral on first Sunday of the month, handing out flyers calling for accountability from priests, bishops, and hierarchy. Many respond positively, taking flyers and giving encouragement with words like "I wish I could do what you're doing."

CHURCH REFORM: Anonymous or underground **newsletters** have been used in numerous social-change movements. Try this method of giving "voice to the voiceless."

## 9. NEWSPAPERS AND JOURNALS

*"Journals and newspapers, both legal and illegal, constantly recur throughout the history of social and political conflicts as media for advancing the views and causes which their publishers espouse."*

HISTORICAL: In **World War II**, during the Nazi occupation of Europe, "illegal [anti-Nazi] **newspapers and news sheets** were . . . widely published and circulated" in Norway, Denmark, the Netherlands, and Poland, much to the dismay of the occupiers, who were unable to stamp them out.

CONTEMPORARY: Many **Church reform groups** have newspapers, journals, or websites to inform members and post upcoming events.

## 10. RADIO, TV, PRESS CONFERENCES, CDS, CELL PHONES, AND THE INTERNET

*All of these have become instruments of nonviolent protest and persuasion. Vivid stories, photos, art, and information can be distributed widely through CDs. The Internet has become a powerful vehicle, not only for disseminating ideas but for social-change organizing.*

HISTORICAL: **Czechoslovakia, 1968:** After the Soviet invasion, clandestine radio and TV **broadcasts** urged opposition to the occupation. "They called for specific acts of resistance, warned against violence, and urged peaceful discipline in the struggle." ✠ Dr. Martin Luther King and his staff used **press conferences** to issue calls to action, respond to attacks, and gather support.

CONTEMPORARY: Groups like Move On use the **Internet** to rally tens of thousands into peaceful anti-globalization and antiwar actions. Most Church reform groups now have websites. ✠ Barbara Blaine, SNAP president, raised public consciousness about clerical sex abuse by appearing on ***The Oprah Winfrey Show*** and other talk shows to advocate for sex abuse survivors and to describe her own experience of molestation by a Catholic priest. ✠ **November, 2004:** Voice of the Faithful held a **press conference** at the Washington meeting of the U.S. Conference of Catholic Bishops to urge inclusion of the laity in the governance and guidance of the Church. ✠ The "Mass Immediate Response" mechanism uses **cell phone text-messaging** to encourage thousands of people at a time to call specific congressional offices with a message of concern about an issue.[9]

## 11. SKYWRITING AND EARTH-WRITING

*Use words, symbols, and materials to convey information to large groups of people. Skywriting includes carrying a large banner behind a plane. In earth-writing, materials like rocks or shrubs are arranged on hillsides or mountains to spell out a message or a symbol.*

HISTORICAL: **Boston Common, Oct. 15, 1969:** Skywriting displayed a large nuclear disarmament symbol in the sky over the rally against the war in Vietnam.

CHURCH REFORM: What would it be like if, at a prayer vigil outside a cathedral calling for women's ordination, a message suddenly **appeared in the sky** saying, "Ordain Women Now!"?

## Group Representations

*Usually includes sending a few individuals from the broader direct-action group who take a message to an individual or institution that can make change.*

## 12. DEPUTATIONS

*Groups of self-selected or chosen people meet with officials judged responsible for a grievance.*

HISTORICAL: In about **1890**, a group of Chinese taxpayers sent a **deputation** to the capital with documents showing repeated malpractice by local tax collector. "The first delegation was a failure and the members received fifty blows of the bamboo and a fine. The second deputation was successful; the tax collector was fired and banned from future government employment."

CHURCH REFORM: **Deputations** to Church leaders from Church reformers often are quite small. Leaders can use this as a reason not to take them seriously. What about a group like Voice of the Faithful organizing carefully among its thirty thousand members and sending a **deputation of three thousand prayerful Catholics** to a meeting of the U.S. Catholic Bishops, asking, for example, that sessions making decisions affecting the faithful (such as those concerning sex-abuse policy) be videotaped and made available to the laity? Or that the bishops set up a lay review board not limited to clergy sexual abuse? (A deputation of three thousand would involve mobilizing only about 10 percent of VOTF's members.)

## 13. MOCK AWARDS

*"Satirical 'awards' may be presented to opponents in order to publicize grievances and perhaps appeal to the recipient of the 'honor' to correct the grievance."*

HISTORICAL: In **1969** in Massachusetts, "while hearings on industrial pollution were in progress, the Boston Area Ecology Action campaign presented to the Boston Edison Company a **Polluter of the Month** award."

### 14. GROUP LOBBYING

*Personal visits to government representatives in order to influence their voting or to get them to speak out on an issue. May take on the character of a nonviolent action if lobby group is large or does some symbolic action in conjunction with the lobbying.*

CONTEMPORARY: SNAP and its allies have **lobbied several legislatures** to reduce or eliminate the statute of limitations around sex abuse. ✠ **Catholic bishops** frequently have taken constituents to lobby state and national legislatures about moral issues like abortion.

### 15. PICKETING

*Picketing tries to persuade others to take or refrain from certain actions. Can be done standing, sitting, or walking back and forth, and may include leafleting and carrying placards. Pickets may or may not try to talk with others to promote their cause.*

More than 400 delegates of the Freedom Democratic party assembled from over 40 counties met in Jackson, Mississippi, to chose 68 delegates as alternatives to the National Democratic Committee.

HISTORICAL: **Washington, Jan. 10, 1917**: **White House was picketed** for first time in history by **woman suffragists** pointing to President Wilson's lack of commitment to votes for women. HISTORICAL: **Picketing used widely** in labor union strikes, civil rights and anti-war movements, and in many other justice and peace efforts.

CONTEMPORARY: SNAP has **picketed US bishop meetings** on several occasions, sometimes holding photos of sex-abuse victims. ✠ **Pro-life groups** frequently picket and leaflet **abortion clinics**. (Contrary to the public perception, even though some of these actions have been verbally violent, the majority have been nonviolent, prayerful, and respectful.)

### 16. MOCK ELECTIONS

*Elections not officially sanctioned by authorities and designed to question or make a point about an election or electoral process.*

HISTORICAL: **Mississippi, fall 1964**: Prevented from voting, the Freedom Democratic Party staged **its own "election,"** inviting all Mississippians to vote on ballots listing all the regular candidates plus the FDP candidates. The latter won among the nearly eighty thousand "voters." This tactic instructed participants in voting mechanics, sparked their interest in challenging their disenfranchisement, and showed their considerable strength.

CHURCH REFORM: The laity, contrary to ancient Church tradition, have no role in **selecting their bishops**. Hold **a mock election** when a bishopric becomes vacant to assert the laity's right to have a voice.[10]

*Means by which participants in nonviolent action express their viewpoint through symbolic action. Very popular over the years. Methods listed here do not exhaust the possibilities.*

### 17. DISPLAYS OF FLAGS AND SYMBOLIC COLORS

*A common type of nonviolent protest, often motivated by or arousing deep emotions.*

HISTORICAL: **India, 1928**: **Black flags** were hoisted by nationalists who were refusing to cooperate with a British parliamentary commission. ✤ **South Vietnam, Sept. 9, 1963**: Students campaigning against the corrupt Diem government in South Vietnam "tore down the government flag and hoisted the **Buddhist flag**, after which more than one thousand students were arrested." ✤ **Paris, Jan. 16, 1969**: Helicopter called in to remove a 15-by 6-foot **anti-Vietnam-war flag** found flying from the top of the 240-foot central spire of Notre Dame Cathedral.

CHURCH REFORM: **What kinds of flags**, flown from what buildings, would convey an urgent message of Church reform?

### 18. WEARING OF SYMBOLS

*Wearing on one's person some item of clothing, a color, a badge, a flower, or the like.*

HISTORICAL: **Denmark, 1942:** Students wore **red, white, and blue caps** similar to those worn by the RAF to symbolize opposition to the Nazi occupation. In **Norway**, for the same purpose, people wore **paper clips** ("hang together") on their lapels. ✤ **World War II**: Some non-Jews in Denmark, France, and elsewhere in Europe wore the **yellow star** voluntarily after the Nazis made it compulsory for Jews. ✤ **South Vietnam, 1963**: During the Buddhist struggle against Diem, Vu Van Mau, the foreign minister, resigned and **shaved his head** in protest against the regime's violent policy. Many professors and students did the same.

U.S. Convener Joe Murray of
www.rainbowsashmovement.com

CONTEMPORARY: **United States: "The Rainbow Sash Movement"** encourages individuals to wear rainbow-colored sashes or lapel symbols to show solidarity with homosexuals and disagreement with Church policy toward them. ✤ **Los Angeles, 2005:** Two hundred sexual-abuse victims and supporters, demonstrating outside the Cathedral of Our Lady of the Angels, **tied crime scene tape** around themselves and the Church's perimeter.

CHURCH REFORM: What **dramatic symbol or symbolic act** would express the depth of our sorrow at the Church's dysfunctionality and our determination to work for needed reforms?

## 19. PHOTOS

*Photos can have a profound effect on people when these images not only depict a wrong but evoke emotions of outrage or sorrow.*

HISTORICAL: During the **Vietnam war, a powerful photo** that aroused much anti-war feeling was a front-on shot of a young Vietnamese girl running naked down a road with her arms outstretched, fleeing a napalm attack.

CONTEMPORARY: **Providence, R.I., May 31, 2005**, Cathedral of Saints Peter and Paul: In an appeal to Catholic bishops to acknowledge their failure to address the sexual-abuse crisis as it unfolded and the inadequacy of their efforts to protect children, abuse survivors and their supporters stood in front of Cathedral Plaza, holding **message signs and large photos** of survivors at the age when priests abused them, while members of the clergy and hierarchy processed by on their way to the installation of Thomas Tobin as the new bishop of Providence.

16th Street Baptist Church — movement headquarters
*Birmingham Civil Rights Institute photo*

## 20. PRAYER AND WORSHIP

*May be conducted so as to convey moral condemnation and protest, as well as to ask God's help and guidance in moving ahead with a nonviolent campaign.*

HISTORICAL: **Gandhi's mass rallies** often left large blocks of time for prayer. ✝ **South Africa, 1950s: Prayer** was an important part of the antiapartheid Defiance Campaign, such as when five thousand Africans welcomed released prisoners, then prayed for the success of the campaign. When police ordered them to disperse, women at Ixopo fell on their knees in prayer, and the police stood around helplessly. ✝ **Dr. Martin Luther King, Jr.,** and his partners commonly used Churches as a base for their demonstrations against racial segregation. The **worship services**, filled with gospel hymns, prayers, and powerful preaching, played a profound role in keeping up participants' morale and building a sense of faith-based solidarity in the common struggle. ✝ **Birmingham, 1963:** After worshiping at Pilgrim Baptist Church, two thousand African Americans came out, faced the police, and **knelt in silence as a minister prayed:** "Let them turn their water on. Let them use their dogs. We are not leaving. Forgive them, O Lord." ✝ **Vietnam, 1963:** During Buddhist struggle against the Diem regime, Catholic priest and university rector Fr. Cao Van Luan led students to **pray at a Buddhist pagoda** in symbolic protest against the government. **Vietnam, 1966:** Buddhist erected **altars** in the middle of streets and protestors carried family altars in front of tanks.

CONTEMPORARY: **Washington, Jan. 20, 2005:** At the demonstrations to protest President Bush's inauguration, 21-year-old Mennonite student Justin Shenk knelt between obscenity-yelling, flag-burning protesters and police in riot gear and prayed for peace, in spite of being repeatedly doused with pepper spray by police. Soon, protester after protester followed his lead, until thirty were kneeling near him. ✠ **1999 through 2007:** FutureChurch developed prayer services and organizing resources that **sparked some three to four hundred celebrations per year** across the United States. They centered around Mary of Magdala's vital leadership role in the early church—not as a public sinner, as so often portrayed by the church, but as the "apostle to the apostles" and the first witness to the Resurrection.

CHURCH REFORM: What about adapting the **"worship-action" model** of the U.S. civil rights movement for Church reform efforts? ✠ Hold a well-publicized worship service in which all the **male language** in the liturgy ("he," "him," "man") is changed to female language.

## 21. DELIVERING SYMBOLIC OBJECTS

*Protestors may deliver "an object which symbolizes a grievance or an objective" to an office or official associated with the issue.*

HISTORICAL: **Chicago, June 3, 1960:** The Woodlawn Organization (organized by Saul Alinsky) **piled rats** on the steps of city hall to pressure Mayor Daley to deal with slum conditions. ✠ **London, Oct., 1961:** To protest Soviet nuclear-weapons tests, Committee of 100 supporters brought hundreds of **bottles of milk** labeled in red, "Danger—Radioactive," and left them in front of the Soviet Embassy. ✠ **Washington, 1963:** In his campaign, President Kennedy had promised to eliminate discrimination in federally assisted housing "with the stroke of a pen," by signing an executive order to that effect. When nothing had happened two years after he took office, the Congress of Racial Equality sent **thousands of bottles of ink** to the White House, telling the press that maybe the President's pen had run dry.

Soulforce members attempt to deliver a coffin representing gay, lesbian, bisexual and transgender people who have committed suicide to the delegates of a church convention in New Orleans, 2001.

CHURCH REFORM: Diocese refuses to release information on sexually abusive priests. Reform group **sends hundreds of keys** "in case they need help in unlocking their files." ✠ To protest the **European-only art** inside most Catholic Churches and the lack of welcome this shows for people of color, multiracial group of Catholics takes **icons of saints of African, Hispanic, Asian, Native American, and other ethnicities** and hangs them on the wall of the diocesan cathedral, holding a worship service of repentance and racial healing. ✠ Have a long line of sexual-abuse survivors and supporters, each **carrying a large stone**, march to the diocesan cathedral and pile the stones on the front steps. Hold a press conference explaining that the stones symbolize how survivors have been given only stones when they have sought real nourishment from bishops (for example acknowledgment of hierarchical responsibility for covering up crimes by reassigning unbalanced predator priests, opening Church records, naming credibly accused priests, or marshaling resources to lobby for tougher laws against abuse). "Jesus said, 'What parent, when his child asks for bread, would give that child a stone?' We've asked for bread and received only stones."

## 22. SYMBOLIC LIGHTS

*Candles, lanterns, or torches used at campaign meetings, events, or marches.*

HISTORICAL: **South Africa, June 1953:** Supporters of the anti-apartheid movement lit candles, lanterns, or bonfires outside their homes as a symbol of their determination to keep the spark of freedom alive.

## 23. SYMBOLIC SOUNDS

*"Oral or mechanical sounds may be used to convey ideas in a conflict situation."*

HISTORICAL: **France, May 1917:** Soldiers being sent to the front and being massacred because of poor leadership, marched to the trenches **baaing "in imitation of lambs being led to the slaughter."** ✠ **Czechoslovakia, Aug. 26, 1968: Church bells and sirens** sounded throughout the whole country to protest Soviet troops and tanks sent to quash the democratic movement.

CHURCH REFORM: There are many occasions where **quiet "baaing" by lay people** would show their opposition to being treated like sheep.

## Pressure on Individuals

*Nonviolent pressure may be directed at specific persons or groups associated with a particular injustice.*

## 24. "HAUNTING" OR "SHADOWING"

*"As a means of reminding officials of the immorality of their behavior . . . and of the determination and fearlessness of the population, volunteers may sometimes follow and 'haunt' officials everywhere they go, thus constantly reminding them" of the issue being addressed."*

HISTORICAL: **India, 1928:** During the Bardoli campaign, volunteers **followed officials** wherever they went, including camping outside their bungalows. Those arrested were replaced by others.

### 25. FRATERNIZATION

*Get close to officials on a friendly basis, but with the objective of convincing them to change. The point may be to convince authorities that what they are doing is wrong or to develop the kind of personal relationships wherein officials will see that demonstrators mean them no harm. Groups using this method must be especially cautious not to become co-opted.*

HISTORICAL: In the **Philippine movement** to depose President Marcos (described in Chapter 2), nonviolent actionists often **approached army troops** sent to repress them in a friendly way, talking to them, bringing them water, and offering them flowers.

### 26. VIGILS

*Like picketing, but more solemn, often of a religious character, and frequently maintained over a longer period of time, sometimes around the clock.*

Philippine activist fraternizing with soldier, 1986.

HISTORICAL: **Netherlands, 1917:** Dutch women **vigiled for weeks** outside the building where the new constitution was being drafted, seeking a clause granting women's suffrage. The clause was not inserted, but women got the vote soon after. ✚ **Vykom, India, 1924–1925:** Untouchables were prevented from using a main road passing a high-caste Brahman temple and had to use long detours to move from place to place. Anti-untouchability campaigners mounted at barricades across the road a **day-and-night prayer vigil** which lasted fourteen months. In the rainy season, flood waters reached the shoulders of the protesters. Police guarding the barricades had to use boats. When barricades were finally removed, "reformers declined to walk forward until the orthodox Hindus changed their attitude. After sixteen months, the Brahmans said, 'We cannot any longer resist the prayers that have been made to us, and we are ready to receive the untouchables.' The case . . . [assisted] in the removal of other restrictions elsewhere and strengthened the cause of caste reform."

CHURCH REFORM: What we call "vigils" are often of fairly short duration. What about an **open-ended vigil** to call attention to a reform issue? Do any of us feel strongly enough about an injustice in the Church to stand in a prayer vigil for sixteen months, as did the Vykom untouchables and their allies?

## Drama and Music

*Nonviolent protest and persuasion may be expressed also in drama and through music. There are many possible variations of the methods described here.*

## 27. HUMOROUS SKITS, STREET THEATER, AND PRANKS

*When done in protest, these can have an important role in non-violent action.*

HISTORICAL: **Philadelphia during Vietnam war:** FBI agents entered the Powelton Village neighborhood, home to many antiwar activists, wrote down license numbers, and took other intimidating actions. Activists responded by dressing in long trench coats and snap-brim fedoras and **writing down the license numbers of FBI cars**. The government harassment stopped. ✚ **New York, 1970s:** Augusto Pinochet's government tortured political opponents in the Chilean sailing ship, *La Esmeralda*. When the ship docked in New York during the tall ship extravaganza, crowds of unknowing tourists lined up to tour the beautiful, square-rigged vessel. Churchmouse, an **ecumenical group of Christians, did street theater on the dock** in front of the line of tourists. They built a mock gallows, tied one of their members to it, and then rigged cables from him to a simulated electric, hand-cranked generator. Another member, dressed in Chilean military garb, cranked the handle to simulate the electric-shock torture that had been used on the ship. As the prisoner screamed in pain, curious tourists took leaflets that explained the situation and urged them not to go on board. Many expressed sympathy and left the line.

CONTEMPORARY: On Nov. 14, 2005, fifty members of the Women's Ordination Conference, in a "ministry of irritation," used ten-foot puppets in a **street theater skit** in front of the national bishops' conference meeting to "witness . . . for women's ordination in a renewed priestly ministry."

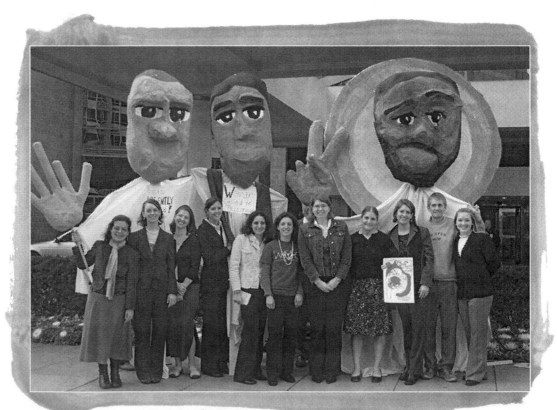

Women's Ordination Conference, November 2005.
*Image courtesy of www.womensordination.org*

## 28. PERFORMANCES OF PLAYS AND MUSIC

*Under certain conditions, these can be a form of nonviolent protest.*

HISTORICAL: **Nazi-occupied Norway, Jan. 1943:** Nazis executed citizens of Trondheim who resisted the German presence. In protest citizens **refused to attend** Nazi-promoted light plays. Instead, thousands attended performances of heavy and somber music by Norwegian composers like Grieg and Gresvik. ✚ Many **playwrights**, including Arthur Miller of the United States and Athol Fugard of South Africa, have used their plays as a way to examine and protest social injustices.

CONTEMPORARY: Recently, **the play *Doubt*,** which deals with an alleged case of clerical sex abuse, was on stage in New York and received good reviews.

## 29. SINGING

*Singing can be a means of nonviolent protest, including "singing while an unwanted speech is being made; singing national or religious songs and hymns; rival vocal programs to compete with boycotted ones organized by the opponent; singing while engaged in a march, civil disobedience, or some other act of opposition; and singing songs of social and political satire and protest."*

HISTORICAL: **The spirituals of enslaved African Americans** (such as "Nobody Knows the Trouble I've Seen") played a vital role in their struggle for freedom. Hymns ("Precious Lord, Take My Hand") and freedom songs ("Ain't Gonna Let Nobody Turn Me 'Round") sustained, consoled, and energized the **U.S. civil rights movement**.

Jennifer Flowers and Christopher Gabardi in John Patrick Shanley's *Doubt.*

CONTEMPORARY: Pete Seeger's **songs** ("Where Have All the Flowers Gone") have inspired and continue to inspire people in the labor, peace, human rights, and environmental movements as has the work of Joan Baez, The Beatles, Bob Dylan, and Holly Near. Modern rap and hip-hop music expresses political dissent and the "marginalization, brutally truncated opportunity, and oppression"[11] Blacks face in urban America.

## 30. FILMS

*Many films have raised consciousness about social conditions, lauded courageous fighters for justice, or highlighted the need for social change.*

HISTORICAL: Just a few of the dozens **of films** that could be mentioned: *Gandhi* (superb film on the career of this pioneer in active nonviolence); *Mr. Smith Goes to Washington* (Jimmy Stewart as a new congressman confronts corruption in the Capitol); *To Kill a Mockingbird* (Gregory Peck portrays a southern lawyer who defends an innocent Black man and descends into a maelstrom of racial hatred).

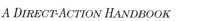

CONTEMPORARY: The **Catholic sexual-abuse crisis** is being examined through films like *Our Fathers* and *Holy Watergate*.

CHURCH REFORM: Reform group invites a crowd and shows a film on the sexual-abuse crisis **on the wall of the diocesan cathedral**.

## Processions

*"Some of the best-known methods of nonviolent protest and persuasion are forms of processions, i.e., people walking or marching."*

### 31. MARCHES

*"A group of people walk in an organized manner to [or around] a particular place which is regarded as intrinsically significant to the issue involved. The duration of the march may vary from an hour or two to several weeks, or even longer. Posters and banners may or may not be carried, and leaflets may or may not be distributed to bystanders."*

HISTORICAL: **Japanese-occupied Korea, 1919:** Three thousand Koreans **marched** to different foreign consulates in Seoul to demonstrate Korean opposition to Japan's rule. ✠ **India, 1930:** Imperial Britain created a salt monopoly and imposed an excessive tax on salt, which fell most heavily on the poor. **Gandhi led the Salt March** in which thousands of Indians marched to the beach at Dandi where they made salt themselves in violation of the law. ✠ **Cuba, 1956:** In reprisal for a peoples' uprising against the repressive dictator, Batista, soldiers seized a fourteen-year-old boy, tortured and killed him, and then dumped his mangled body on an empty lot. Two days later, forty Cuban women dressed in black, with the slain boy's mother in the lead, **marched out of the Church of Dolores**, praying quietly in unison and fingering their rosaries. Over their heads they carried a large white banner saying, **"Stop Murdering Our Sons."** As they marched toward Santiago's city hall, more and more women joined them, until over one thousand were marching. When a Jeep full of soldiers blocked their way, training machine guns on them, the women waited quietly as more and more women continued to join them. When the soldiers waded into the procession to break it up, the women, silently and without offering any physical resistance, opened aisles, let them through, then closed ranks again. The soldiers gave up and part of the march continued to city hall and to the offices of several newspapers, where the women left petitions, demanding an end to the terror. This was "the first public act to signal the beginning of organized civic resistance on a broad and effective scale in Cuba."

CONTEMPORARY: **Manchester, N.H., Sept. 2003:** New England Call to Action **marched with sexual-abuse victims** demanding the ouster of Bishop John McCormack, accused of reassigning unstable, abusive priests while an aide of Cardinal Bernard Law in Boston.[12]

### 32. PARADES

*Parades are different from marches in that it is the parade itself, rather than the place to which it is processing, that conveys the point.*

*Parades often use large banners and are accompanied by costumes, musical bands, and other activities.*

HISTORICAL: **Washington, 1913:** The first **women's suffrage parade** in the nation's capital had eight to ten thousand participants, including many senators and representatives and their wives. Participants were assaulted by opponents, but the resulting press coverage and political uproar only put further attention on the women's demands. ✠ **Japan, 1960:** Students protesting the U.S.-Japanese Security Pact used **three parade variations:** the zig-zag or snake-like parade, the hand-in-hand parade, and the centripetal parade, in which marchers start from many points but converge on a central symbolic spot.

## 33. RELIGIOUS PROCESSIONS

*Differ from marches or parades by their religious quality, and may involve carrying religious pictures, crosses, statues of the Virgin, singing religious songs, or including participation by clergy and other religious.*

HISTORICAL: **St. Petersburg, Russia, Jan. 9, 1905:** Columns of Russians, led by Fr. Gapon, **processed** toward the Czar's Winter Palace singing hymns and carrying icons, religious symbols, the Russian national flag, etc. The Czar's troops fired on them, killing about one hundred and wounding another three hundred. "This action alienated the peasants from the Czar and aligned most of the intelligentsia and even conservatives against the regime."

CHURCH REFORM: What about a procession to the diocesan office, asking that a **Diocesan Council be elected**, similarly to Parish Pastoral Councils?

Gandhi leading the Nationalists on the Salt March, India, 1930.

## 34. PILGRIMAGES

*Involves one or more people walking to a point of significance, such as a Church or government building. Often takes several days, weeks, or even months. A form of moral condemnation which brings a message to people, does penance for some deed or policy, or provides a means of rededication to a cause.*

HISTORICAL: **India, 1947:** Gandhi makes a **walking tour** pilgrimage through Bengal "in an effort to persuade Hindus and Muslims to halt their murderous rioting and to live together peacefully."

## 35. MOTORCADES

*A parade in cars with posters or banners, usually moving at a very slow speed.*

HISTORICAL: During the **1968 Poor People's Campaign** in Washington, many participants arrived from distant parts of the country in **motorcades**, "advertising" the purpose of the campaign on the way.

CONTEMPORARY: According to **Amnesty International**, the Mexican government was failing to investigate or prevent the terrorizing of young women in Ciudad Juarez and Chihuahua, where nearly three hundred women had been murdered or disappeared over the last ten years. In 2004–2005, as part of its global **"Stop Violence Against Women Campaign,"** Amnesty organized a **cross-country Caravan of Justice** public-education tour through the United States to Mexico. This helped to compel the U.S. Congress to intervene and pressure the Mexican government to take action.

CHURCH REFORM: Even a relatively **small group of people in a well-publicized motorcade**—stopping at towns, holding rallies, and giving speeches in churches, schools, town halls, and assemblies—can help put the spotlight on an injustice and inspire people to act.

## Honoring the Dead

### 36. MOURNING

*Mourning for a person or persons who have died can turn into a ceremony honoring what they stood for and calling for rededication to the cause for which they gave their lives. But ceremonies of mourning need not be restricted to honoring the dead.*

HISTORICAL: **Philadelphia, 1765:** In the struggle against the Stamp Act, all the **flags** flew at half-mast and the city's **bells tolled all day** when the tax stamps arrived by ship. ✚ **Argentina, 1943:** Opponents of Peron's dictatorship wore **black symbols of mourning**, such as black neckties, arm-bands, lapel ribbons, veils, or headcloths. This gave new strength to the anti-regime movement.

CONTEMPORARY: **April, 2005:** Soulforce members nationwide **wore black armbands to Mass** as a symbol of faithful dissent for weeks after the election of Cardinal Ratzinger to Pope. They pointed to his direct involvement in key documents opposing birth-control information and condoms to the poor, denying ordination to women as a matter of papal infallability, and supporting the "justifiable denial of human rights" to gay, lesbian, bisexual and transgender people.

CHURCH REFORM: **For what do we mourn** in the Church and how might we express it? What about Cardinal Law who, after resigning because of his complicity in sexual-abuse cover-up, was given a generous stipend and apartment in Rome, the position of Archpriest of St. Mary Major, and continuing roles in various important Vatican congregations?

## 37. MOCK FUNERALS

*These protests illustrate how certain policies and actions are "killing off" some important principle or stance.*

HISTORICAL: **Newport, R.I., Nov. 1, 1765:** To protest the British-imposed Stamp Act, which was about to become law, the Sons of Liberty staged a **"Grand Funeral of Freedom,"** carrying a coffin marked "Old Freedom." Speeches and street theater lamented the death of liberty under the heel of tyranny and oppression. ✠ **Montgomery, March 1965:** To call attention to the deaths of ten civil-rights workers, demonstrators took **ten caskets** in a funeral procession of automobiles from Lowndesboro, Alabama, to the state capital.

CHURCH REFORM: What **funeral procession** would memorialize people or principles harmed by Church policies or practices? Sexual-abuse victims who have committed suicide? Laity whose gifts have died for lack of use? Gay and lesbian Christians who have attempted or committed suicide because of the Church's condemnation?

Soulforce mock Jazz Funeral, New Orleans, 2001.

## 38. HOMAGE AT BURIAL PLACES

*Visits to a burial place by large groups of people or by a series of individuals or small groups can be nonviolent action when the dead has been associated with the moral issue being raised.*

HISTORICAL: **Budapest, Dec. 4, 1956:** In response to the second Soviet attack on the capital, "Hungarian women, many black-veiled, **walked to the tomb of Hungary's Unknown Soldier . . .** where they heaped flowers on the tomb. They sang the old Hungarian national anthem with these lyrics: 'Shall we be slaves? / Shall we be free?/ That's the question, what's your answer? / In God's great name we swear, we swear / No more shall we be slaves—no more.'"

## Public Assemblies

## 39. ASSEMBLIES OF PROTEST OR SUPPORT

*Gatherings of people at places appropriate to the issue. These range from small meetings to well-organized protests involving thousands.*

HISTORICAL: **Philadelphia, 1773:** During the tea boycott, **eight thousand people gathered** to direct the captain of a tea ship to leave for England at once. ✠ **South Africa, 1952:** As part of the Defiance Campaign against apartheid, **open-air mass meetings** were held in several cities. ✠ **Norway, World War II: Children gathered at railway stations** and sang patriotic songs to show solidarity for arrested teachers being transported to prison camps in northern Norway. ✠ **Berlin, 1943: Non-Jewish wives** of some two thousand Jewish men arrested by the

The author speaking in front of the White House in a campaign protesting U.S. military aid to Pakistan, 1971.

*LOVE IN ACTION*

Nazis **assembled** determinedly in front of the building where the men were being held, in spite of threats and intimidation from the Gestapo and SS. After a week, the Gestapo released the husbands, ending the practice of sending intermarried Jews to the death camps.[13]

CONTEMPORARY: **Georgia, 2006:** Twenty-two thousand people attended the annual anti-war protest at the **School of the Americas** in Fort Benning. ✚ **Boston, 2005:** Fr. Walter Cuenin, the popular pastor of **Our Lady Help of Christians Catholic Church**, was outspoken in supporting social justice, women's ordination, gays, and divorced Catholics. When the Archdiocese forced his resignation, more than one thousand Catholics, Protestants, and Jews, organized by the parish's laity, marched to the chancery in protest.

## 40. TEACH-INS

*Differs from a public protest in that various "viewpoints are represented both among the speakers and those attending, and the speakers may be high-level specialists on the subject." Generally, the idea is not just to protest, but also to present a variety of viewpoints so people can make up their own minds. Part of the dynamic is confrontation of opposing viewpoints, questioning of speakers, and discussion from the floor.*

HISTORICAL: **Widely used in anti-Vietnam war protests,** especially in England and the United States.

CHURCH REFORM: **Invite bishops** and their supporters to appear on the platform with abuse survivors and persons who believe the bishops should be held responsible, morally and legally, for the abuse crisis.

School of Americas protest, November 2006, Fort Benning, Georgia.
*photo © 2006 by Linda Panetta*

## 41.  WALK-OUTS

*A person or group expresses protest "by walking out of a conference, assembly, meeting or discussion before it has been adjourned."*

CHURCH REFORM: Catholics gather in many venues for many purposes. When might a **walk-out** to protest a Church policy, action or lack of action be appropriate?

## 42.  SILENCE

*Silence may be a primary method of showing disapproval or may be combined with other methods, such as a silent march.*

HISTORICAL: **Madrid, 1962:** To show solidarity with striking workers, women went to Madrid's central square and **showed "silent support" by walking quietly** around the plaza singly or in pairs. ✚ **Berkeley, Calif., 1964:** When student proponents of the "Free Speech Movement" were heckled by their peers, who threw eggs and lighted cigarette butts at them, the Free Speech advocates **responded with simple silence.** After forty-five minutes, the hecklers left.

CONTEMPORARY: **Washington, November 2002:** After three faithful Catholics and members of Soulforce were denied Eucharist at the Bishops' Mass, they proceeded to the hotel where the bishops were staying and **knelt silently in the lobby, hands out to receive communion.** They were arrested for trespassing, and their case went to trial. The judge refused to impose any penalty for their actions, and praised them

Soulforce members requesting communion from the
Catholic Bishops, November 2002, Washington, D.C.

for their courageous faith. Ultimately, the judge cited their witness as a reason she retired from the court and went to seminary.

## 43. RENOUNCING HONORS

*Renouncing an honor conferred on—or offered to—a person or a group by the body against which a campaign is being directed is a powerful protest method. This may involve renunciation of medals, titles of honor, honorary offices, or resignation from prestigious societies closely identified with the opponent's cause. This may show self-sacrifice for a cause and may in itself weaken the authority of the conferring body.*

HISTORICAL: **India:** During the independence struggle, "Sikh soldiers in large numbers **returned their war medals,** and thousands of other Indians relinquished their [Britain-conferred] titles. The famous poet Rabindranath Tagore surrendered his title of British knighthood." Gandhi himself returned to the British Viceroy a gold medal and two other medals given him for his humanitarian work in South Africa. He said: "Valuable as these honors have been to me, I cannot wear them with an easy conscience."[14]

## 44. TURNING ONE'S BACK

*This is a way of showing silent disapproval of persons responsible for or allied with the injustice.*

HISTORICAL: **U.S. colonies, 1771:** When Governor Hutchinson of Massachusetts Bay Colony proclaimed a day of prayer and fasting, he included a call for thanks for the "continuance of our privileges." This implied support for British policies. Only one minister read the proclamation, doing so with evident embarrassment, because many **congregants turned their backs** or left.

Prayerful, convicted witnesses like this vigil for peace can be as transformative for participants as for those they hope to persuade.
*Photo by Ryan Rodrick Beiler, courtesy of www.sojo.net*

# ACTIONS TO SUSPEND COOPERATION AND ASSISTANCE

*Though their noncooperation, nonviolent activists deliberately withdraw support from the person, activity, or institution against which the campaign is directed. "The actionists conduct their struggle by reducing or ceasing their usual cooperation, or by withholding new forms of assistance, or both . . . Noncooperation involves the deliberate discontinuance, withholding, or defiance of certain existing relationships."*

## SOCIAL NONCOOPERATION

*This involves "refusal to continue normal social relations . . . with persons or groups regarded as having perpetuated some wrong or injustice, or to comply with certain behavior patterns or social practices." Since this method sometimes has been accompanied by hatred and vindictiveness, great care must be taken to emphasize loving outreach to ostracized persons in hopes their behavior will change.*

*The introduction to this chapter notes that it is possible to use so-called "nonviolent" methods for destructive ends. Social boycotts, for example, have been used to isolate Jews or other minorities. India, where so much creative nonviolence has been pioneered, is also the country where untouchables have been socially boycotted for centuries. Again, only methods that are prayerful, that have worthy objectives, and that express goodwill toward opponents can be true expressions of gospel nonviolence.*

## Ostracism of Persons

### 45. SOCIAL BOYCOTT

*Refusal to carry on usual social relations, a tactic widely used in direct-action campaigns. Sharp cites some thirty cases from many countries and eras. Here are just three:*

HISTORICAL: **England:** Labor unions have used a social boycott called "Being Sent to Coventry" by **not relating to workers** who refuse to take part in strikes. ✚ **Providence, R.I., 1769:** To enforce its campaign **against importing British goods,** the town meeting socially boycotted anyone who refused to sign or obey the campaign's regulations. In the same year in Boston, the names of violators of the economic boycott of British goods were printed and published. ✚ **Colonial India, 1930s:** Nationalists used the **social boycott** against Indians who refused to join the independence movement. "In Gandhi's view, the social boycott could be permissible or not, depending upon the spirit and manner in which it was carried out. Boycotted persons, for example, should be supplied with food, water, and medical care, and the boycotters should not feel hatred or vindictiveness against those boycotted; instead, the attitude should be sorrow, concern, and hope that they would rejoin the community by stopping their help to the British government."

## 46. SELECTIVE SOCIAL BOYCOTT

*"Instead of a social boycott being total or near-total, it may be restricted to one or more particular types of relationship . . . Thus shopkeepers or traders may be willing to speak to occupation troops but refuse to sell them anything."*

HISTORICAL: **Port Said, Egypt, 1956:** During the Suez invasion, street peddlers **refused to sell** to British or French soldiers and merchants in the European section and simply closed down their shops.

---

# Noncooperation with Social Events, Customs, & Institutions

---

## 47. SUSPENSION OF SOCIAL AND SPORTS ACTIVITIES

*Cancellation or refusal to arrange these activities.*

HISTORICAL: **Norway, World War II:** Occupying German troops tried to normalize relations by offering to play sports with Norwegians, but the latter refused. When the Nazi troops tried to join Norwegian sports clubs, the Norwegians declined. The **"sports strike"** spread throughout Norway and became a model for noncooperation by other institutions.

## 48. BOYCOTT OF SOCIAL AFFAIRS

*Refusal to attend banquets, receptions, parties, concerts, and the like.*

HISTORICAL: **Occupied Denmark, World War II:** Danes refused to attend concerts of German military music.

## 49. STUDENT STRIKE

*Students temporarily refuse to attend classes or selectively boycott specific lectures.*

HISTORICAL: **St. Louis, May 1935:** Students at the Belleville Township High School **refused to attend classes** to protest the firing of teachers for political reasons. ✠ **Guatemala, June 1944:** "The noncooperation movement which toppled Guatemalan strongman Jorge Ubico . . . began with a **strike of students** at the National University." ✠ **Netherlands, 1940–41:** "Students at Delft and Leiden went on **strike** to protest against the dismissal of Jewish professors." ✠ **New York, Jan. 3, 1964:** Nearly a half million pupils **stayed home** to protest *de facto* racial segregation and bad conditions in schools. During a similar strike the following year, "freedom schools" were held for children protesting the regular school system. ✠ **United States, Vietnam War:** Student strikes were so widely used to protest the war that a **National Strike Information Center** was set up at Brandeis University.

A female demonstrator offers a flower to military police on guard at the Pentagon during an anti-Vietnam war demonstration. October 21, 1967.

*Photo by S. Sgt. Albert R. Simpson*

CHURCH REFORM: What would have happened if students at **Jesuit universities** had gone on strike in 2005 when **Fr. Thomas Reese** was forced to resign as editor of *America* magazine?

## 50. SOCIAL DISOBEDIENCE

*Not following the rules, customs, regulations, or practices of social institutions.*

HISTORICAL: **Fourth Century Catholic Church:** Cardinal John Henry Newman, regarded as the Church's intellectual leader of the age, wrote that it was the **open, sustained dissent of the laity**, not the efforts of bishops and Church authorities, which saved the Church from the Arian heresy. While Church synods and councils were upholding the heresy, the laity "strenuously and persistently dissented from the [heretical] doctrine in the face of excommunication, persecution, even martyrdom."[15] One of the methods they used was to refuse to take Communion from an Arian bishop. ✠ **India:** Persons who oppose untouchability "have often **deliberately fraternized with untouchables**, defying both the religious taboo and social customs." Gandhi adopted an untouchable as his own daughter. ✠ **United States: Civil-rights freedom riders** were among those who violated racist taboos by collaborating across racial lines.

CONTEMPORARY: **Philadelphia, 2002:** A member of the Synod Preparatory Commission on Moral and Social issues continued to speak out and raise questions about commission procedures despite being told by the priest chairman that he was **not being "a team player."**

CHURCH REFORM: In dioceses where bishops have been complicit in clergy sexual abuse or have done or said other things with which people strongly disagree, what would it be like if groups of people **declined to stand** when the bishop enters a Church for a ceremony or other occasion?

## 51. WITHDRAWAL FROM SOCIAL INSTITUTIONS

*Members either resign or stop participating in the body without actually cancelling membership.*

HISTORICAL: **Concord, N.H., 1840:** Deacon Amos Wood, a member of the antislavery movement, **withdrew temporarily from his Church** to attend a meeting of antislavery worshipers.

CONTEMPORARY: **Philadelphia, 2002:** The Commission on Moral and Social Issues was one of several preparatory commissions making recommendations to an upcoming Synod. Two commission members, an African American nun and a White layman, developed thirty-nine recommendations for addressing racism in the archdiocese. When only one was included in the final report, the layman **resigned from the commission**, saying he could not with integrity put his name on such an emasculated document.

## 52. NONOBEDIENCE AND DISGUISED DISOBEDIENCE

*Participants ignore or do not comply with laws, rules, edicts, or instructions, especially where there is no direct enforcement. This disregard takes place without blatant defiance. Resisters give the disobedience the thinly disguised appearance of obedience.*

HISTORICAL: **Chungking, China, 1942:** When the government closed ice cream shops and banned the sale of coffee and soda pop, the fancy Sing Sing Café reopened under the name Sing Sing Kitchen and **served ice cream** on tables laden with plates, water glasses, and silverware to give the appearance of dessert after a full meal. "Soda pop was served in soup plates and had to be eaten with soup spoons." ✚ **Europe, World War II:** Thousands listened to **illegal broadcasts** from Britain in spite of threats of punishment by German occupiers. ✚ **Germany, World War II:** When the Nazi government banned jazz music, defiant "**jazz enthusiasts changed the names** of American jazz numbers to innocent-sounding German titles." Thus "Organ Grinder Swing" became *"Hofkonzert im Hinterhaus"* (Court Concert in the Back Yard), "Tiger Rag" became *"Schwartzer Panther"* (Black Panther). "One such number was even played by the official *Wehrmacht* (German Army) band." ✚ **Occupied France, 1942:** Until forcibly stopped, Jews required by Nazis to **wear the yellow star either declined to do so**, wore it the wrong way, wore several stars instead of one, or added inscriptions to the star.

CONTEMPORARY: **United States:** In many Catholic Churches, parishioners who strongly object to **sexist language in the liturgy** practice "disguised disobedience" by adding more inclusive wording to Scripture readings (such as, "brothers and sisters" instead of just "brothers," "humanity" instead of "mankind"). They also may rework the words of the regularly recited creed (". . . For us [not 'for us men'] and for our salvation, he came down from heaven . . . and became human [not 'man']

. . . We believe in the Holy Spirit . . . with the Father and the Son, She [not 'He'] is worshiped and glorified. Who [not 'He'] has spoken through the prophets.")[16] ✠ **Worldwide Catholicism:** Survey after survey shows that the majority of Catholic laity not only disagree with the Church's teaching on **birth control** but disobey it themselves by using contraception.

## Withdrawal from the Social System

### 53. STAY-AT-HOME

*The population as a whole, or a large portion thereof, remains at home for a set period, usually one or two days, rather than going about their normal activities. "In addition to reducing the chances of 'incidents,' it may serve to demonstrate to the opponent the degree of unity and self-discipline among the population."*

HISTORICAL: **South Africa:** Stay-at-homes were used frequently in the antiapartheid struggle to protest repressive legislation or to mourn the dead of the liberation struggle.

### 54. SANCTUARY

*An individual or group important to the opponent withdraws to a place where they cannot be touched without violation of religious, moral, social, or legal prohibitions. Churches, temples, and other places considered holy have often been used for such refuges.*

HISTORICAL: There are a **multitude of examples** from Church history, the antiwar movement, Islamic history, etc. (See Sharp, pages 204–210.)

### ECONOMIC NONCOOPERATION

*"Economic noncooperation consists of a suspension of or a refusal to continue specific economic relationships." This can involve refusing to undertake certain economic relationships, such as buying, selling, or handling of goods and services, or the restriction or suspension of labor that supports such relationships.*

## Action by Consumers

### 55. CONSUMER BOYCOTT

*Consumers refuse to buy certain goods or services. Some reasons for such a boycott: (1) price is too high, (2) objection to the conditions under which the goods or services were produced, (3) item isn't equally available to all, (4) item may symbolize a wider grievance, (5) item may be seen to have immoral qualities, (6) consumers object to how profits from sales will be used.*

HISTORICAL: **Widespread use throughout history**, such as in 1859, when Russian peasant serfs expressed hatred for serfdom by starting a temperance movement to deprive the Czarist state of revenues from its vodka monopoly; 1934 boycott of "immoral" films by Protestants and the Catholic League of Decency; 1936 New York housewives boycott of meat to protest high prices; 1955–1957 bus boycott in Montgomery to end segregated seating; 1957 bus boycott by sixty thousand Black South Africans to protest hike in fares; 1960 selective patronage campaign by 250,000 Philadelphians against the Tasty Baking Company to obtain equal job opportunities for African Americans.

Philadelphia minister Leon Sullivan led the successful boycott against Tasty Baking Company.

### 56. POLICY OF AUSTERITY

*The voluntary giving up of luxuries to demonstrate the depth of the boycotter's feelings, deepen their commitment, and negatively impact the goods being boycotted.*

HISTORICAL: **Colonial United States, 1765–1766:** Mourners **radically simplified their funeral practices**, which had involved buying costly imported British goods like fancy scarves and gloves and distributing them to mourners.

## Action by Holders of Financial Resources

### 57. REFUSAL TO PAY FEES, DUES, AND ASSESSMENTS

*People deliberately refuse to pay monies that, under other circumstances, they would feel an obligation to pay.*

CONTEMPORARY: Many faithful U.S. Catholics, appalled by the clerical sexual-abuse crisis and the complicity of Church leaders, have expressed their feelings by **cutting back on their regular contributions** to the Church. Unable to make their voices heard by Church authorities and lacking decision-making power to influence Church policy, many laity feel that withholding their money is the only way to express their distress and to send a message to Church leaders. However, one of the factors making people reticent to take such a step is their concern that such financial withholding will harm valid Church programs which need support, such as services to the poor. ✚ **Ohio:** Voice of the Faithful groups in Cincinnati and Dayton began a "Your Choice, Your Vote" effort to encourage members to **contribute directly to the charities** that the archdiocesan annual fund supports and to inform the archbishop why they are not contributing to his annual appeal. Long Island VOTF initiated a similar program called "Our Dollars Make a Difference."

### 58. CREATION OF ALTERNATIVE FINANCIAL MECHANISMS

*When people are unwilling or uneasy about putting their funds in the hands of institutions judged to be morally suspect or not financially transparent, they sometimes have created alternative mechanisms to convey their money to recipients judged to be more worthy.*

CONTEMPORARY: Some Catholics, distressed about various matters in the Church, including the sex-abuse crisis, have put their regular contributions into **alternative funds,** which are used for Church building repairs, programs for the poor, and other efforts.

*"The strike involves a refusal to continue economic cooperation through work. It is a collective, deliberate, and normally temporary suspension of labor designed to exert pressure on others"* so they will be more amenable to the strikers' demands. To be effective, the number of strikers must be large enough to interfere with or make impossible the work of their economic unit. Strikes mostly happen over wages, but they can be organized for noneconomic reasons as well.

### 59. PROTEST STRIKE

*Work is stopped for a specific period of time—a minute, a day, a week—in order to make clear the workers' feelings about the issue at stake. This demonstrates to employers that workers can strike longer or more effectively if necessary.*

HISTORICAL: There have been innumerable strikes by workers and labor unions throughout history. ✚ Because of their generally low salaries, **Catholic schoolteachers** and administrative workers sometimes have gone on protest strikes.

CHURCH REFORM: If the leaders of a diocese do something egregiously wrong, a **protest strike by employees**, possibly joined by other Catholics, might be a strong way to express concern.

### 60. PROFESSIONAL STRIKE

*Salaried or self-employed persons go on strike.*

HISTORICAL: **United States, 1700s: Lawyers often suspend their practices** in the context of nonviolent campaigns. When British-approved tax stamps were required to be used in colonial courts, "lawyers frequently responded by suspending practice." ✚ **Russia, 1905:** Lawyers responded to the massacre on "Bloody Sunday" by "**refusing to appear in court** and by issuing a formal protest against 'the pitiless hand of the government.' "

CHURCH REFORM: Could theologians strike when a colleague is silenced without due process?

### 61. SYMPATHETIC STRIKE

*Workers strike, not to improve their own situation but in sympathy for fellow workers.*

HISTORICAL: **Norway, 1924:** Paper-mill workers struck in sympathy with locked-out transport workers. ✚ **Guatemala, 1944**: Railroad workers struck in support of striking students at the National University, working to overthrow the dictator president, Jorge Ubico.

CHURCH REFORM: When **Catholic teachers go on strike** over a grievance, Church secretaries and maintenance workers could also walk out.

## 62. DETAILED STRIKE

*Workers stop work one by one until the employer has to ask about their grievance and demands.*

HISTORICAL: **New York, 1914:** In the clothing workers' strike, "the pant-makers struck one day, the vest-makers the next, and finally the coat-makers, as a means of demonstrating the workers' power."

## 63. SLOW-DOWN STRIKE

*Rather than leave their jobs, workers "deliberately slow down the pace of their work until the efficiency is drastically reduced."*

HISTORICAL: **Commonly used by slaves** in the pre-abolition South, causing tremendous financial losses to owners.

CHURCH REFORM: A possible method for **Church employees** who may be afraid to do a full strike, but can do a slowdown to seek redress of their grievances.

## 64. "SICK-IN"

*Workers call in sick, en masse.*

HISTORICAL: **United States, pre-abolition South:** Much illness among slaves, but also much **feigned sickness,** with "sick" slaves often in a ratio of one sick to seven well. Sick on Saturday, but rarely on Sunday. More sickness when most work required. ✚ **China, 1952:** Strikes were forbidden, and the regime urged workers to work harder. Outwardly, workers seemed animated with zeal, but their "illnesses" caused noticeable **reduction in quantity and quality of work**. Workers formed long lines outside clinics, and doctors generally authorized a few days of leave. Factory absenteeism sometimes reached 20 percent.

Sit-down strike at Fisher Body plant in Flint, Michigan during the strike of 1937.
*Photo by Sheldon Dick*

## 65. LIMITED STRIKE

*Workers do most of their usual work, but put forth marginal effort, sometimes by refusing to work overtime or on certain days.*

HISTORICAL: **St. Petersburg, Russia, 1905:** Workers **introduced the eight-hour day** by simply stopping work eight hours after they reported for duty.

# NONVIOLENT INTERVENTION

*These methods differ from protest and noncooperation in that participants actually intervene in the situation. Nonviolent intervention can aim at preventing something undesirable from happening, or it can be to encourage something positive to occur. It can be used defensively (such as to thwart something an adversary does) or offensively (to carry the struggle into the opponent's own camp). Because of the disruption of power relations or behavior patterns often associated with intervention, it can be more challenging or threatening than other methods. If successful, success is likely to come more quickly "because the disruptive effects of the intervention are harder to tolerate or withstand for a considerable period of time. For example, intervention by a sit-in at a lunch counter disrupts more immediately and completely than would, say, picketing or a consumers' boycott, though the objective of each of these actions is to end racial discrimination."*

*Change caused by intervention is usually through the mechanisms of "accommodation" or "necessitation" discussed in the introduction to this chapter. In those instances, defenders of the status quo change without being convinced they ought to do so. However, sometimes these actions can contribute to the opponents' "conversion," so that they come to see not only the necessity of change, but its rightness.*

## Psychological Intervention

*Rather than physically standing in the opponent's way, this method relies more on exerting moral or psychological pressure on an opponent.*

### 66. THE FAST

*Jesus said, "When you fast . . ." not "If you fast . . ." Depriving oneself of normal sustenance is a way to exert moral pressure to advance nonviolent change. Fasts can be undertaken for a set period of time, an indefinite period, or until death. Fasts can be total (no food or water) or fluids only. The following are only three examples of the hundreds that could be given.*

HISTORICAL: **Ireland: St. Patrick (ca. AD 390–461)**, the great evangelizer of Ireland, "once **fasted against King Trián** to compel him to have compassion on his slaves. On another occasion, he fasted three days and three nights against the Pelagian heresy in a city to compel the inhabitants to become orthodox." ✚ **United States, 1774:** When the British government decreed the closing of the port of Boston on June 1, 1774, Thomas Jefferson, Patrick Henry, and several others proposed and got adopted a resolution for **"a day of fasting, humiliation, and prayer** . . . to turn the hearts of the King and parliament to moderation and justice." The fast day was very successful and crystalized the colony's revolutionary spirit. ✢ **Sicily, 1950s and 1960s:** When a child died of malnutrition, **Danilo Dolci**, the so-called "Sicilian Gandhi," decided to **fast until money was received** for relief of the starving.

## 67. NONVIOLENT AGGRAVATION

*The goal is to stop objectionable behaviors by making a nuisance of one's presence.*

HISTORICAL: **United States, 1850s:** Slave hunters hired to capture fugitive slaves and return them to their masters faced nonviolent aggravation by antislavery activists who put up public **posters, describing the slaver** and giving his name and unconscionable mission. The activists also asked landlords not to house slave hunters. When the kidnappers went out on hunts, "two resolute, unarmed men" would **follow them**, observe their every movement and point them out to others. One antislavery newspaper suggested that "He should not have one moment's relief from the feeling that his object is understood, that he cannot act in secret, that he is surrounded by men who loathe his person and detest his purpose, and have means at hand to prevent the possibility of success."

CHURCH REFORM: If this method were combined with sincere prayer for the person, could it be a way to **call attention to a Church official** who has done something atrocious?

Sicilian activist Danilo Dolci

### Physical Intervention

*This involves interference created by people's physical bodies, especially by entering or refusing to leave some place where they are not wanted or from which they have been prohibited.*

## 68. SIT-DOWN

*Participants sit down on a road, in a room, or at some other symbolic location and refuse to leave. Can be for a limited or indefinite time period. Can be spontaneous or planned ahead. Sometimes used to halt ordinary traffic or military vehicles or to keep workers or officials from entering their place of work.*

HISTORICAL: **Washington, Vietnam War:** Quakers who wanted to do a peace march around the White House were halted by a police officer who threatened to use tear gas or a baton on the protesters if they continued. The Quakers politely replied that they needed to consult God's Spirit, sat down, and held a silent meeting for worship. After a few minutes, they arose, saying they felt called by God to go forward. The officer reiterated his threat. They responded, "We know you're tired and only doing your job, but we believe God is asking us to do this." With that, they stepped off the curb, at which point the policeman said, "Okay, come ahead," and let them proceed.

CONTEMPORARY: **Los Angeles, June 27, 2005:** During 10:00 AM Mass at the cathedral, SNAP member James Robertson **handcuffed himself to the chair** used by Cardinal Mahony to protest the cardinal's handling of the clergy sex-abuse scandal.

## 69. SIT-IN

*"The interventionists occupy certain facilities by sitting on available chairs, stools, and occasionally on the floor . . . with the objective of disrupting the normal pattern of activities."*

HISTORICAL: **Chicago, 1969–70:** African American children were forced to attend a segregated Black school. In the nonviolent campaign, parents **sent their children to the school nearest their homes**. The teachers tried to ignore them, but even though the children sat at their desks in a very orderly manner, a great controversy erupted. When Black parents invaded the offices of the school board and mayor, the segregated school was abolished. ✚ **U.S. civil rights movement:** Sit-ins were widely used, especially after Black students from North Carolina Agricultural and Technical College sat in at **Woolworth's lunch counters** in Greensboro, N.C. Their nonviolent behavior in the face of verbal abuse, jailings, beatings, and having catsup poured on their heads galvanized much wider use of nonviolent direct action across the South. Within seven months, at least seventy thousand Blacks and their White allies had participated in nonviolent direct action. Some thirty-six hundred people were arrested.

Ronald Martin, Robert Patterson, and Mark Martin added momentum to the civil rights movement with their sit-in at Woolworth's lunch counter, 1960.
*UPI photo*

*LOVE IN ACTION*

CHURCH REFORM: What about a well-publicized and carefully planned **sit-in at the financial offices** of the U.S. Conference of Catholic Bishops urging the bishops to adopt a policy in accord with the statement of Fred Hofheinz, religion director at the Lily Foundation: "It is of paramount importance for every diocese in the nation to prepare and widely circulate, at the soonest possible moment, a comprehensive, clear, lucid, understandable, transparent, and brutally honest financial accounting to the people."[17]

## 70. STAND-IN

*Participants continue standing in an orderly, quiet manner when refused service or something else due them.*

HISTORICAL: **U.S. civil rights movement:** When refused admission to movie theater, Black activists and White allies **kept standing in ticket lines**, thus preventing other sales while showing determination to be treated equally. The swimming pool at New Jersey's Palisades Amusement Park was integrated by similar means, despite participants being beaten by park guards and arrested by police.

CONTEMPORARY: **St. Paul, Minn., May 15, 2005:** When about one hundred people were **denied Communion** because they were wearing rainbow sashes or ribbons to show support for gay and lesbian Catholics, they returned to their seats. However, instead of sitting or kneeling, they **remained standing for five minutes with their hands cupped** as a symbol of their continuing desire for the sacrament.

CHURCH REFORM: In cases where Catholics have been unjustly barred from receiving Communion, might a **longer-lasting nonviolent stand-in** have a positive effect?

## 71. PRAY-IN

*Persons enter, or attempt to enter, a church, synagogue, or mosque from which they've been barred by custom or policy in order to participate equally in religious services. Also used when people have been barred, not from the church as a whole, but from some aspect of the liturgy.*

HISTORICAL: **United States, 1848: Frederick Douglass** urged all Black Christians to abandon separate Black Churches and to attend White ones in a massive pray-in. ✚ **Philadelphia, 1830s:** Angelina and Sarah Grimké, new converts to Quakerism, insisted on **sitting with the Black worshipers** in the Meeting House. When scolded by more established Friends, they replied: "While you put this badge of degradation on our sisters, we feel it is out duty to share it with them." ✚ **U.S. civil rights:** Blacks seeking admission to segregated White Churches did a **"kneel-in"** at their front doors.

CONTEMPORARY: **Rockford, Ill., May 15, 2005:** Bishop Doran forbade the VOTF affiliate to meet on Church property. For two years the group tried unsuccessfully to meet with the bishop and get permission. On Pentecost Sunday, more than seventy VOTF **members dressed in**

**red attended Mass** in St. Peter's Cathedral and occupied the back pews. At the end of Mass, knowing it's not permitted, they held a VOTF business meeting, beginning by joining hands and saying the "Our Father" and "Hail Mary." On Tuesday and Wednesday, they flooded Bishop Doran's office with respectful phone calls to ask for a meeting.

CHURCH REFORM: When officials at a parish refuse to be open about financial matters, church members **hold a prayer vigil in his office**, demanding respectful treatment, release of all financial information, and a full financial report to the membership.

## 72.  CALL-IN

*A "call-in" may be organized to convey a message activists have been trying to deliver. This involves having dozens, hundreds, or thousands of people call an office or other location connected with the issue. This "clogging" of phone lines may be done at the same hour, on the same day, or over a period of days.*

## 73.  NONVIOLENT INTERJECTION

*Participants place their bodies between groups who may be in contention or where one group is being attacked by another.*

HISTORICAL: **Boston, 1851:** An escaped slave had been arrested and brought to court. A large group of free Blacks entered the court, milled about, **hid the slave** among them, rushed him out of the room, and started him on the journey to Canada.

CONTEMPORARY: **1983:** Nonviolent activists organized **Witness for Peace (WFP),** a U.S.-based organization set up to send volunteers to Nicaragua to stand between the Nicaraguan people and the contras who

Demonstrators against the Vietnam War erect religious symbols on New Jersey railroad tracks to block trains carrying weapons to an ammunition ship, 1972.

were attacking them. WFP has evolved into a group doing nonviolent witnessing in many parts of Latin America and the Caribbean. ✠ **China, 1989:** The image of a Chinese citizen who placed his body in front of a tank to protect demonstrators became famous worldwide.

## 74. NONVIOLENT OBSTRUCTION

*In this case, participants use their bodies as a physical obstruction.*

HISTORICAL: **Hungary, 1956:** Several hundred unarmed men and women **blocked factory gates** when police and army officers came to arrest three members of the workers council. The officers finally left without the men. ✠ **Philippines:** Demonstrators prevented troop movements by **standing in front of soldiers** and tanks during the campaign to overthrow President Marcos. (See detailed description in Chapter 2.) ✠ **Sunakawa, Japan, 1956:** Ten thousand Japanese peace activists **occupied a site intended for a U.S. air base** until building plans were abandoned.

CONTEMPORARY: **Pro-life demonstrators** frequently have placed themselves between abortion staff and the clinics where **abortions** are performed, sometimes sitting in front of the doors. Nonviolence training has kept most of these blockades peaceful and prayerful, in spite of some media coverage to the contrary.

## 75. NONVIOLENT OCCUPATION

*May be used to consolidate a nonviolent invasion or land seizure.*

HISTORICAL: **Milan, Italy, AD 385:** The Roman Empire's government ordered **Bishop Ambrose** to surrender a church building to Arian Christians. Although the church was surrounded by troops, the bishop

Two hundred sexual-abuse victims and supporters at a nonviolent occupation of the Cathedral of Our Lady of the Angels, 2005.
*Image courtesy of www.cta-usa.org and www.futurechurch.org*

continued to occupy it and, risking imprisonment or death, held masses for five days. Finally, the government withdrew the order and the troops.

CONTEMPORARY: **Boston, 2005:** When Archbishop Sean O'Malley decided to **close more than sixty Boston parishes and schools, parishioners in eight of them occupied their parish buildings,** seeking to reverse O'Malley's decision. (Laity occupied one parish for eight months!) The archbishop set up an external review committee and, upon its recommendation, agreed to allow five of the parishes to remain open and to re-open one that had been closed. In early June, concerned that protestors might occupy Presentation School in Brighton, the archbishop cancelled the last two days of school, causing parents to charge that he was "locking out" children. In response protesting parents, children, and supporters **occupied the "Oak Square" traffic circle** in front of the school, camping out with tents, supplies, and protest signs, one calling the location "O'Malleyville." At one point they were joined by a Boston mayoral candidate, two state representatives and a city councilor. The parents proposed that the school be sold to the Presentation School Foundation (PSF), which would use the building for various preschool, afterschool, and summer programs for children, plus adult education and other social services. Stung by the criticism, the archbishop reversed his decision and, for the first time, entered negotiations with PSF, and agreed to pursue selling PSF the school.

CHURCH REFORM: In extreme cases (such as where a diocese is closing inner-city parishes and schools, claiming lack of funds, but where the diocese has large land or real-estate holdings) a reform group might consider **occupying** such real estate to call attention to these as possible sources of funding.

## 76. CIVIL DISOBEDIENCE

*This is "a deliberate, open, and peaceful violation of particular laws, decrees, regulations . . . which are believed to be illegitimate for some reason." The justification often given is that people have an obligation at times to disobey human laws in obedience to "higher" laws. Generally, such a step is taken only after all other recourse has been exhausted.*

HISTORICAL: **North American colonies: Merchants** expressed opposition to the Stamp Act by refusing to use stamped papers and documents. ✚ **India independence campaign, 1930–31:** "Civil disobedience . . . included the making and public sale of salt in violation of the law, the sale and reading in public of prohibited and seditious literature, defiance of bans on parades and meetings, [and] disobedience of ordinances and police orders." ✚ **Washington, 1965:** In Washington State, many Native Americans depended on fishing for their livelihood. When the State Conservation Department imposed restrictive regulations in violation of Treaty provisions, the tribespeople committed **"fish-ins," by fishing without licenses.** A few hundred Native Americans were involved at first, but their numbers swelled to thousands who did "fish-ins" on a half-dozen rivers.

CONTEMPORARY: **Natick, Mass., Dec. 2004:** On Christmas eve, parishioners participated in a **round-the-clock occupation** of Sacred Heart parish to protest the Boston archdiocese's decision to close eighty-two parishes. The protestors were arrested and charged with trespassing.

## Social Intervention

*Social Intervention involves "methods which take the form of direct intrusion in social behavior patterns, social occasions, and social institutions."*

### 77. ESTABLISHING NEW PATTERNS

*New ways of behavior that positively contribute to establishing new social patterns.*

HISTORICAL: **U.S. anti-slavery movement, 1830s:** In the Northern United States, it was not customary for Whites to **associate with Blacks,** even freed slaves. Sarah Grimké, a Quaker, got the Anti-Slavery Convention to adopt a resolution: "It is the duty of abolitionists to identify themselves with these oppressed Americans, by sitting with them in places of worship, by appearing with them in our streets, . . . by visiting with them at their homes and encouraging them to visit us, receiving them as we do our White fellow citizens." In several cities, Black and White abolitionists did **"walk-alongs"** in which they simply walked the streets with persons of the other color. Sometimes they paid a heavy price: In Pendleton, Indiana, a Quaker doctor who had hosted Frederick Douglass was driven out of town by a mob. ✠ **India, 1930s:** Gora, a prominent man born a high-caste Brahman, organized **inter-caste and interreligious dining** on a mass scale.

CHURCH REFORM: What would it be like if a group of clergy, religious, and laity covenanted together **never to address each other or Church officials with terms that reflect inferiority/superiority,** such as "Your Eminence," "Monseigneur," or "Reverend Father." Their slogan might be that of Pope Gregory the Great, who commented on ecclesiastical titles by saying: "Away with these words that increase vanity and weaken love."

### 78. SPEAK-IN

*Participants go to a meeting, church service, or other gathering and act in a way not normally done, sometimes actually interrupting the meeting.*

HISTORICAL: **England, 1649:** George Fox, founder of Quakerism, was often pummeled, arrested, and imprisoned for his **frequent interruptions of Church services** and his speeches outside "steeplehouses" to departing worshipers. ✠ **Concord, N.H., 1841:** After failing to win permission to speak in a Congregational church, abolitionist Stephen Foster rose during the services and denounced it for upholding slavery. Congregants threw him down the stairs and had him arrested for disturbing public worship.

## 79. ALTERNATIVE SOCIAL OR RELIGIOUS INSTITUTIONS

*Without abandoning an institution that reformers critique, participants set up a similar institution alongside it. This provides an additional venue where people can practice their convictions more freely and which may be seen as having greater integrity. The new institution may or may not challenge the old one. It may simply serve as an outlet for people frustrated by the practices of the old institution. However, by providing a substitute, no matter how quietly it is offered, the new institution can point out the inadequacies of the old and invite people to think about new ways of doing things.*

HISTORICAL: **English Catholicism, 1600s:** Only twenty-two years before Mary Ward's birth, the Council of Trent ordered bishops to make sure all nuns were cloistered and wore habits. Contrary to the Church's established regulations, Mary Ward organized the Institute of the Blessed Virgin Mary (IBVM), a non-enclosed religious community in which the **sisters wore conventional garb, visited prisoners, and taught the poor.** Initially, Rome gave the institute temporary approval, but a special commission sent to investigate it described Ward as "a former Poor Clare nun of a masculine cast of mind" and recommended that the institute be suppressed. Pope Urban VIII did so in January, 1631. Ward was formally accused by the Inquisition of being "a heretic, schismatic, and rebel to the Holy Church." After her death, however, former members continued to live as non-enclosed quasi-religious. In 1877, Pope Pius IX gave approval to the IBVMs. "By the early twentieth century, it had schools and foundations on every continent, and it continues to this day."[18] However, it wasn't until 1909, 224 years after Mary Ward was born, that the IBVMs were allowed to call her their foundress. ✢ **United States, 1800s:** Slaves themselves set up **secret, illegal schools** and went from house to house at night to tutor students. Abolitionists established schools for slaves, sometimes with an integrated enrollment. (In breaking up one such school, a grand jury in Lexington, Kentucky, argued that it would enlighten "the minds of those whose happiness obviously depends on their ignorance.") Rev. John Fee, an abolitionist who never carried weapons, created integrated schools in Kentucky, even though he frequently was mobbed and one school was burned down. ✢ **Occupied Norway, 1942:** In an effort to take control of religion, Vidkun Quisling, the Nazi-appointed head of state, made himself head of the Norwegian Evangelical Lutheran Church, to which 97 percent of the population belonged. The bishops and 93 percent of the clergy resigned from the Church. Most of their parishioners followed them into alternative worship services.

**Mary Ward**
Unknown artist, 1621, English Institute of the Blessed Virgin Mary, Augsburg. National Portrait Gallery, London

CONTEMPORARY: **Philadelphia and suburbs:** A small faith community, the **Margaret Roper Forum** was founded in 1967 by Catholics distressed at the poor quality of adult and children's education in their parishes. Currently with a five-county membership of seventy families who elect a guiding executive board, the Forum provides children's (K–12) and adult education, liturgies (with visiting priests), service to the poor, and social-action opportunities. The curriculum for children's education complies with archdiocesan religious curriculum guidelines and prepares children for the sacraments. ✠ **Indianapolis:** When the diocese closed and then demolished St. Bridget's Church, **parishioners continued their worship in a field** across the street. Eventually, they moved their Catholic community into an Episcopal Church nearby and continued their worship.

CHURCH REFORM: In parishes where some of the parishioners feel great frustration, what about a group of them continuing to attend Mass, but **organizing a separate worship group or faith community** in someone's home, possibly learning from the experience of the Margaret Roper Forum? (For more information, its website is www.mrforum.org.) The danger of this veering off into schism, which no faithful Catholic would desire, can be avoided—or at least minimized—by doing everything quite openly, following diocesan guidelines (such as on children's education), and encouraging members to stay active in their own parishes.

> "The pope has a ministry, but he is not the Church; he is not God. We have to relate to him and be adults in our faith and continue on the journey. The big institutions only change if there is strong pressure at the bases. The Church, divine and human, will only change if there is a coherent force, universal at the bases."
>
> (Brazilian Bishop Pedro Casaldaliga, after the election of Pope Benedict XVI, quoted in *Call to Action* newsletter, May 2005, page 1).

## 80. SEEKING IMPRISONMENT

*Normally, imprisonment is a secondary consequence of civil disobedience. At times, however, arrests and jailing may be sought to encourage increased resistance by others, express solidarity with already arrested associates or to press for their release, show lack of fear of arrest, clog courts or fill prisons, or obtain wider publicity for an issue.*

HISTORICAL: **Occupied Norway, 1942:** When Quisling ordered the teachers at Stabekk school to be arrested, "teachers who had been absent went to the prison and **demanded to be arrested** also." ✠ **Jackson, Miss., 1961:** In connection with a wave of freedom rides against racial segregation on buses, the Congress of Racial Equality (C.O.R.E.) organized a **"jail-in"** to fill the jails and drastically increase the expense and inconvenience of holding so many prisoners.

# NOTES

1. Gene Sharp, *The Politics of Nonviolent Action* (Boston: Porter Sargent, 1973), 109–445.

2. Gene Sharp, *Waging Nonviolent Struggle* (Boston: Porter Sargent, 2005), 50.

3. Gene Sharp, "Beyond Just War and Pacifism," *The Ecumenical Review*, Vol. 48, Number 2, April 1996, 235ff.

4. Ibid., 235.

5. Gene Sharp, *The Politics of Nonviolent Action* (Boston: Porter Sargent, 1973), 117. From this point on, so as to avoid hundreds of footnotes, only material quoted from sources other than *The Politics* will be footnoted. Any quotations *not* footnoted can be found in *The Politics*, between pages 117–445. Many of the historical examples are from the same section of Sharp's book.

6. Adam Roberts, *Civilian Resistance as a National Defense* (Harrisburg: Stackpole Books, 1968), 210.

7. The whole nonviolent campaign is described in detail in Richard Taylor, *Blockade: Guide to Nonviolent Intervention* (Maryknoll: Orbis Books, 1977).

8. The dramatic story of this turnaround (and Murray's hierarchy-imposed suffering for his beliefs) can be found in Robert McClory, *Faithful Dissenters* (Maryknoll: Orbis Books, 2000), 7–24.

9. People for the American Way started using this in May 2005 to prevent shutting down debate on judicial nominees sent to the Senate for confirmation. (PFAW Activist Network e-mail, May 12, 2005).

10. In Acts 1:12–26, the disciples, plus about 120 believers, together choose the successor to Judas. The first-century Church document, the Didache, states: "You [the faithful] must, then, elect for yourselves bishops and deacons." St. Cyprian (3rd century) said: "The people themselves most especially have the power to choose worthy bishops or to reject unworthy ones." For many other references to the laity's role in bishop selection, see Francis A. Sullivan, SJ, "St. Cyprian on the Role of the Laity in Decision-Making in the Early Church," in Stephen J. Pope (ed.), *Common Calling: The Laity and Governance of the Catholic Church* (Washington, D.C.: Georgetown University Press, 2004), 39–49; Association for Rights of Catholics in the Church, "Petition on the Selection of Bishops," May 1, 2005 e-mail.

11. Eric Bennett, "Hip Hop in the United States," in *Africana: The Encyclopedia of the African and African American Experience* (New York: Civitas Books, 1999).

12. *ChurchWatch* (newsletter), Oct. 2003, 7.

13. The film, "*Rosenstrasse*," tells this story very movingly and accurately.

14. M. K. Gandhi, *Nonviolent Resistance* (New York: Shocken Books, 1970), pg. 136.

15. McClory, *Faithful Dissenters,* 40–48.

16. The strongly sexist language in the first paragraph of the otherwise magnificent *Catechism of the Catholic Church* is an egregious example of Church leaders' insensitivity. In this one brief paragraph of 6 sentences and 116 words, the text manages to use sexist terms 21 times, or almost 20 percent of all the words. One might think that the writers were intentionally trying to offend women! The first paragraph reads: "God, infinitely perfect and blessed in *himself,* in a plan of sheer goodness freely created *man* to share in *his* own blessed life. For this reason, at every time and in every place, God draws close to *man. He* calls *man* to seek *him,* to know *him,* to love *him* with all *his* strength. *He* calls together all *men* . . . etc." (emphasis added).

17. "Signs of the Times" section, "Full Financial Disclosure Essential to Church Response to Crisis," *America* magazine, Oct. 14, 2002, 4.

18. McClory, *Faithful Dissenters,* 65. Mary Ward's whole story is told in Chapter 4 of McClory's book.

# Appendix 1
# Love Your Enemies

Jesus' toughest commandment is "Love your enemies." Yet contemporary theologian Miroslav Volf says that it expresses the essence of Christian faith: God has befriended us even though we are God's enemies. Therefore we are called, with God's help, to befriend *our* enemies.

Mahatma Gandhi, a Hindu, recognized both the difficulty and the possibility of love of enemies. "It is no nonviolence," he said, "if we merely love those that love us. It is nonviolence only when we love those who hate us. I know how difficult it is to follow this grand law of love. But are not all great and good things difficult to do? Love of the hater is the most difficult of all. But by the grace of God even this most difficult thing becomes easy to accomplish if we want to do it."[1]

Some people believe this tough commandment doesn't really apply to them. "I don't have any enemies," they claim. But Foy Valentine, a Southern Baptist leader, speaks more realistically when he says:

> Enemies seem to be a fact of life. There are people who see things differently, who want to solve problems in ways that you find unacceptable, or who are just on the absolutely opposite side from you regarding some really important issues . . .The question is: What am I to do with these enemies? Jesus says, "Love your enemies." Christians are sacrificially and aggressively to seek good and not evil for them . . . So what do I do with my enemies? I pray for them. I seek their good. I never rejoice over their misfortune. I help them when they are in need. I work for their peace and welfare. I love them.[2]

In Chapter 3, Step 2, "Prepare Spiritually," we talked about this rigorous commandment. The following are some further suggestions, exercises, and meditations whose purpose is to deepen your ability to love those who oppose you. You may practice them as individuals or in groups. Certainly, you can add to these from the rich life experience of the members of your direct-action group.

## DRAW UPON YOUR OWN EXPERIENCE

Everyone reading this, whether in childhood or later on, has met someone who spoke ill of them, thwarted them, or opposed them in some way. Reflect, individually and perhaps as a group, on how you dealt with the feelings this opposition created in you. Reflect also on those times when you did not give back in kind. What enabled you to return a certain amount of goodwill for ill will? What lessons have time and distance taught? What did that experience teach you that could be used in a campaign for Church reform?

## BLOW OFF STEAM

Locked-down emotions can explode unexpectedly. If your group would find it helpful, set aside time to rant and rave at what bugs you about the Church. You might begin: "This is just a time to let out our feelings without censorship or disapproval. For these minutes, rule one is 'Let it all hang out.' Rule two is 'Feelings just are—criticism of others' feelings is not allowed.' After you've gone crazy for a while, come back to the hard, Jesus-mandated business of trying to love those who oppose us, pray for those who abuse us, and do good to those whose behavior inspires our outrage."

## DRAW UPON SCRIPTURE

✚ Memorize Bible verses that deal with love of enemies.

✚ Pray over Ephesians 2:13–18. Remember a time when you experienced Christ "breaking down barriers of hostility which had kept people apart."

✚ Meditate on 1 Peter 3:8–17. Remember a time when you or someone else returned a blessing for an insult. How did it affect you? How did it affect the other person(s) involved?

✚ Read 2 Corinthians 5:14–21. Think of an opportunity to be an ambassador of reconciliation. Act on it.

✚ Use Romans 12:9–21 to examine your own behavior.

## HOW TO LOVE OPPONENTS: AN EXERCISE

1. List on some newsprint all those who are opposing your reform campaign (a priest? a bishop? a diocesan official? an organization? an antagonistic lay person?).

2. Read out loud the words of Jesus in Luke 6:27: "But I say to you that listen: Love your enemies, do good to those who hate you, bless those who curse you, pray for those who abuse you."

3. Reflect quietly for a few minutes on this verse's meaning for you and your group.

4. Pray aloud for each opponent on the list.

5. Discuss, in light of this verse, some practical ways to show love for these opponents.

6. Agree on one or more practical steps you'll take to implement these ways. For example:

    a. Write your opponent a letter which expresses "the truth in love" in an affirming, reconciling way. Really stretch—express all the affirmative things you can honestly say about the person before listing any criticisms or suggestions.

    b. Write a letter asking them for a photo of themselves, saying that you plan to circulate it among your group members so that each person can pray for them more personally.

    c. Commit to the practice of praying for the opponent every time they come to mind.

## REFLECT ON AGAPE

Reflect on the meaning of this biblical word for love, as described on page 31. Does *agape* help you see how you might love your enemies? Remember that it doesn't mean we have to like our opponents, feel affection for them, or want to be friends with them. It's a choice to show goodwill toward others, even if they come at you with hostility, misunderstanding, disdain, or opposition.

## USE WALL POSTERS

As reminders of what we're about, try putting up powerful quotes on the walls of your meeting room, such as those below:

***BHAGAVAD GITA*** *(Hindu sacred text):* "If you want to see the heroic, look for those who can love in return for hatred."

***CESAR CHAVEZ:*** "I am convinced that the truest act of courage, the strongest act of humanity, is to sacrifice ourselves for others in a totally nonviolent struggle for justice."[3]

***MOTHER JONES*** *(pioneer labor organizer, 1830–1930):* "I abide where there is a fight against wrong."[4]

***HENRY WADSWORTH LONGFELLOW:*** "If we could read the secret history of our 'enemies,' we should find in each man and woman's life sorrow and suffering enough to disarm all hostility."

***SHELLY DOUGLASS*** *(Catholic peace activist):* "The point of nonviolence, after all, is to search for the right and loving thing to do and do it, remaining centered in the truth."[5]

***ABRAHAM LINCOLN:*** "I destroy my enemies when I make them my friends."

**MIROSLAV VOLF** *(contemporary theologian):* "The Christian basis for loving/embracing our enemies is the belief that God loved us so much that he suffered for us, even though we were God's enemies."[6]

**MARTIN LUTHER KING JR.:** "At the center of nonviolence stands the principle of love."[7]

**MOTHER TERESA:** "At the hour of death, when we come face to face with God, we are going to be judged on love; not how much we have done, but how much love we have put into our actions."

**ST. PAUL:** "Owe no one anything, except to love one another . . . Love does no wrong to a neighbor; therefore, love is the fulfilling of the law" (Romans 13:10).

## USE A PRAYER FOR A NONVIOLENT HEART

Try saying together, at the beginning or end of your meetings, a prayer like the following: "O Creator God, pour into us your sanctifying Spirit, that we may express to others the love and example of Jesus. Preserve us in nonviolence of tongue and heart. Help us love those who oppose us. In the face of provocation, be our calm. Energize us to work against injustice and to resist what is wrong, whether in the world or the Church. Strengthen us to accept suffering rather than to inflict it. Loving God, we trust in your sustaining love and power. Bestow on us the abundant grace to fulfill this prayer. Amen."

**Christianity**          *M. P. Wiggins*

Another prayer: "Loving God, in the course of our campaign we are going to run into people who disagree with us, oppose us, even wish us ill. Please help us, in obedience to your Son, to pray for them, to seek their good, to help them when they are in need, and never to rejoice over their misfortune."

As an individual, pray regularly: "Lord Jesus, free me of hatred and disdain. Fill me with your love."

## SAY THE PRAYER OF ST. FRANCIS

*Have group members commit to saying the prayer of Saint Francis daily during the campaign.*

Lord, make me an instrument of Your peace.
Where there is hatred, let me sow love;
where there is injury, pardon;
where there is doubt, faith;
where there is despair, hope;
where there is darkness, light;
and where there is sadness, joy.
O, Divine Master,
grant that I may not so much seek
to be consoled as to console;
to be understood as to understand;
to be loved as to love.
For it is in giving that we receive;
it is in pardoning that we are pardoned;
and it is in dying that we are born to eternal life.

## ADOPT A DISCIPLINE OF RESPECTFUL LANGUAGE

Words are powerful. Creation is the result of God's word. The Incarnation is the Word become flesh. We shouldn't bandy about words irresponsibly. For Saint Thomas, one of the most serious sins was to use words to destroy someone's reputation.

It is appropriate to use forceful language to challenge injustice. Even exaggeration and hyperbole have their place. The problem is when we consistently use language that does not respect the humanity of those who oppose us. We can counter the habit of scornful or generalizing language by practicing respectful language.

For example, rather than lumping the "the bishops" all together, try calling them "our brother bishops." Rather than saying of a stubborn-seeming priest, "He'll never change," try saying, "I pray that the Holy Spirit will give him new light." Such a shift in language can bring a shift in us. New behaviors can create new attitudes. A change in how we speak of others can transform the way we look at them and gradually bring about more compassion in our own hearts.

Ask someone in the group to monitor a meeting to see how many times the words *we, us, they,* and *them* are used. Reflect on these usages at the end of the meeting.

## STRUCTURES OF DOMINATION

In the vast majority of cases, our opponents are not bad people. If they are clergy, they may be trapped by ingrained thought patterns established during their seminary training or long-established ways of doing things. They may be afraid to change. If, as some believe, the laity are oppressed in an oppressive structure run by clerics,[8] "oppressors" may be just as ensnared in the system as are the laity. In any case nonviolence attacks not those responsible for domination but the structures of domination themselves. As Dr. King said, nonviolent resistance "is directed against the forces of evil rather than against persons who are caught in those forces. It is evil we are seeking to defeat, not the person victimized by evil."[9]

In relation with Church leaders, be respectful without being obsequious, assertive without being arrogant, teachable without groveling, conscious of your own gifts without putting down theirs, dialogical without argumentativeness, informed without smugness, strong without being defiant, committed without obstinance, courageous without cockiness, bold without being disrespectful, reconciling and forgiving without losing sight of justice.

# NOTES

1. Mohandas K. Gandhi, quoted in Krishna Kripalani, *Gandhi: All Men Are Brothers* (New York: Continuum, 1982), 78.

2. Foy Valentine, Southern Baptist Convention leader, in the denominational newsletter, *Light*, May 1980.

3. Quoted in Shannon McManimon, *The Way of Peace: Exploring Nonviolence for the 21st Century* (Erie: Pax Christi USA, 2003), 118.

4. Ibid., 61.

5. Ibid., 48.

6. Quoted in the *National Catholic Reporter*, March 14, 2004.

7. Lotte Hoskins, *I Have a Dream: The Quotations of Martin Luther King Jr.* (New York: Grosset and Dunlap, 1968), 97.

8. Professor Paul Lakeland of Fairfield University makes an impressive case for viewing the laity as an oppressed group within the Church. See his book *The Liberation of the Laity: In Search of An Accountable Church* (New York: Continuum, 2003), 186–206.

9. Martin Luther King Jr., "Nonviolence and Racial Justice," *Christian Century*, Feb. 6, 1957, 166.

# Appendix 2
# The Organizer's Checklist

Copy these three pages and tuck them in your back pocket or purse. These checklists serve as handy, condensed reminders of all the steps in a well-organized direct-action campaign. Use them to keep in mind your overall goals, major steps you will need to cover, and responsibilities that must be attended to. The material is covered in greater detail in Chapter 3, so if you need more specific information on certain topics, simply turn to the page numbers indicated.

## The Organizer's Twelve Steps

### 1. DISCERN PERSONAL AND GROUP COMMITMENT

A nonviolent action or campaign takes time, effort, and spiritual energy. Make reasonably sure your group is free enough and motivated enough to meet these demands (pp. 28–29).

### 2. PREPARE SPIRITUALLY

Let your anger drive your intelligence. Transform anger into *agape* love (pp. 29–32).

### 3. ORGANIZE YOUR GROUP

Draw people in. Foster a positive group spirit. Hold effective, prayerful meetings. Divide the work. Keep deepening your understanding of gospel nonviolence (pp. 32–35).

### 4. INVESTIGATE

Get your facts straight. Try to understand the other side. Look for alternative solutions (pp. 36–37).

### 5. STRATEGIZE

Develop a vision. Be clear about your values. Set clear goals. Do a SWOT assessment. Decide on an action plan with SAM objectives. Consider possible direct-action methods (pp. 38–43).

## 6. NEGOTIATE

Negotiate with people who can make the change, not with gatekeepers. Prepare carefully for every meeting. Name a negotiation team. Set the agenda. If negotiations fail, be clear about next steps (pp. 44–51).

## 7. EDUCATE AND BUILD BROADER SUPPORT

Intensify your outreach. Speak to people's values. Try many approaches, including one-on-one conversations (pp. 52–55).

## 8. PREPARE FOR DIRECT ACTION

Do a strategic estimate. Explore direct-action possibilities most likely to achieve your goals. (See the eighty methods in Chapter 4). Write a covenant of nonviolence. Decide on tasks to be done and who will do them. Here is a checklist of the **eight most basic tasks** (pp. 56–59):

❒ Coordination             ❒ Leaflets

❒ Recruitment              ❒ Communications

❒ Media Relations (Press Team)   ❒ Monitors/Peacekeepers

❒ Signs and banners        ❒ Police liaison

Other possible tasks:

❒ Scout the demonstration site and/or route

❒ Family Support and Child Care

❒ Medical (heatstroke in hot weather? injuries?)

❒ Transportation Coordination

❒ Equipment (speakers' podium? sound system?)

❒ Finances/Fund-Raising

❒ Legal advisors/advocates

❒ Water

❒ Singers and song sheets

❒ Food

❒ Nonviolent chants

❒ Photography/Videography

❒ Training

❒ Clean-up

## 9. TRAIN FOR DIRECT ACTION

Use an experienced outside trainer or learn the basics and do your own training (pp. 60–62).

## 10. MAKE A FINAL APPEAL (pp. 63–64)

# 11. TAKE STRONG BUT LOVING DIRECT ACTION

Here is a checklist of direct-action "To Do's"(pp. 65–69)

## *Before the Demonstration* (p. 65)

- ❑ **Coordination:** *Final plans. All responsibilities assigned? Everything fit together? Rally site?*
- ❑ **Recruitment:** *Last phone calls/emails to get maximum turnout.*
- ❑ **Media/Press Team:** *Press releases, calls, interviews. Press spokesperson chosen? News peg?*
- ❑ **Signs, Banners:** *Who'll bring them to the site? Who'll carry them in the demonstration?*
- ❑ **Leaflets:** *Written? Enough copies? Leafleters to pass them out on demonstration day?*
- ❑ **Communications:** *All equipment functioning? Who'll bring to the site? Where set up the PA system? Bullhorns? Cell phones with key people's numbers?*
- ❑ **Monitors/Peacekeepers:** *Touch base and review what they'll do. Covenant of Nonviolence ready? Who will hand it out?*
- ❑ **Police Liaison:** *Phone relevant office(s). Give update on plans as appropriate. Permits in place (if needed)? Be friendly, willing to negotiate nonessentials, but firm about essentials.*

## *On Demonstration Day* (pp. 66–69)

- ❑ **Coordination:** *Make kick-off remarks. Make sure people are positioned effectively. Remember that you are a servant leader.*
- ❑ **Recruitment:** *Get names and contact information from new people. Invite them to future planning and action.*
- ❑ **Press Team:** *Early morning media calls. Press spokesperson? Hand press release to reporters.*
- ❑ **Signs/Banners:** *Bring to the site, get people to carry them.*
- ❑ **Leaflets:** *Leafleters position themselves for maximum traffic. Hand out leaflets with a smile.*
- ❑ **Communications:** *Someone assigned to each piece of equipment. Set up PA system at site.*
- ❑ **Monitors/Peacekeepers:** *Give Covenant of Nonviolence to everyone. Handle any disruptions.*
- ❑ **Police Liaison:** *Introduce yourselves. Give them a leaflet and a copy of the Covenant of Nonviolence. Answer questions. Be friendly and flexible, but clear and firm about your goals, legal rights, and what you intend to do.*

# 12. CELEBRATE, EVALUATE, PLAN NEXT STEPS (pg. 70)

# Appendix 3

# Questions for a Strategic Assessment

Some of the questions below can be answered definitively. Some call for your best estimate based on current knowledge. Some questions may not be able to be answered at all. It's not crucial that every answer be upbeat and positive. The strategic assessment is similar to a military battle plan—you do your best with what you've got. (General Eisenhower didn't have all the answers before he decided to launch the D-day assault on June 6, 1944.)

## QUESTIONS TO ASSESS OUR NONVIOLENT DIRECT-ACTION GROUP

1. **PEOPLE:** How many people are members of our group? How many others outside our group (individuals and institutions) can be counted on to join us, as participants in direct action or as supporters? Who are our "natural allies," (for example, peace-and-justice activists, Catholic Workers, other Church reform groups)? How many are part of a wider circle that would be likely to join the campaign if we can help them understand the issue and what we plan to do? Can we draw in other people who may not want to demonstrate, but who can offer other kinds of support? What organizations might provide people to help? Are there priests or vowed religious who might join if invited? Are there sympathetic people within the power-holding institution who, if reached, would give us covert or even overt support?

2. **OUR GROUP:** Are we working together reasonably well? Do our meetings go smoothly enough to get the necessary work done? Are people taking responsibility for work that needs doing? Remembering that we don't have to be perfect, are there any internal conflicts (personality clashes, rivalries, power struggles, deep disagreements) serious enough to warrant our attention before we move into direct action?

3. **NONVIOLENCE:** What knowledge of and experience with nonviolent direct action do our members and leaders have? Do we now have—or can we acquire—the skills and knowledge needed to do effective direct action? Are we able to channel creatively any anger we may feel into *agape* love? How many of us have received training in nonviolence? How can we get further training?

4. **COMMITMENT:** How deeply do we care about this issue? Where are we on a scale of one to ten (1= extremely weak commitment; 10 = extremely strong dedication)? Do we have a core of people who, all other things being equal, will persevere in spite of sanctions that power-holders may levy?

5. **OUR MESSAGE:** Does our message appeal to values that are widely held by Catholics? By other Christians? By other religious groups? By the public at large? Do we have convincing arguments? Do we have spokespersons who can articulate our message clearly and forcefully?

6. **STRATEGIES:** Do we have group members who have a knack for strategizing? Have we chosen direct-action strategies and tactics that will educate the public by painting a clear, dramatic picture of the injustice and the fallacy of the rationalizations used to cover it up? Are our strategies momentum-building? Do they show a better way to do things?

7. **SPIRIT:** Are we prayerful? Are we being nurtured by worship and the Eucharist? Are we relying on God's guidance and strength? Do we have reason to believe God is asking us to take this next step into direct action?

8. **EMOTIONAL STATE:** Are we psychologically and physically up for this? Do we have enough energy to carry this through? Is anyone exhausted or in burnout and needs to rest? If real sacrifices are called for, are we still ready to go ahead?

9. **COMMUNICATIONS:** Do we have effective ways of communicating with one another, including in emergencies? Are we set up to get our message out to our membership? To the public? To the Catholic population? To key groups? What is our relationship with the media? What coverage can we expect? Do we have any friends or sympathizers in the media? If not, can we cultivate them?

10. **FINANCES:** Do we have—or can we raise— the funds to meet the expenditures direct action will require? Do we have a financially knowledgeable member handling our funds?

11. **STRENGTHS AND WEAKNESSES:** In general, where are we strongest? Where are we weakest and most vulnerable? How can we shore up these areas? Can our strongest qualities be used to highlight where our opponents are weakest and most vulnerable?

12. **WEIGHING:** What are the pros and cons of going forward into direct action? As far as we can estimate, do the pros outweigh the cons? What can we accomplish with the people and resources we have today?

# QUESTIONS TO ASSESS THE POWER-HOLDERS

1. **PEOPLE:** What is the degree of support the power-holders enjoy from Catholics and the population in general? What are the methods they will use to rally Catholics behind them? Who are their natural allies? Which representative(s) of power-holders are likely to respond to us?

2. **SANCTIONS:** What methods could they use to try to dissuade us from acting? Rational arguments? Private rebukes? Getting others to try to talk us out of it? Public attempts to discredit us? Ecclesiastical punishments? Calling security? Getting the police to make arrests? What sanctions have they used in the past against other groups working for change?

3. **COMMITMENT:** On the issue we're addressing, how deeply do the powerholders care about preserving the status quo? Where are they on a scale of one to ten? Are they likely to dig in and try to resist to the bitter end? Or are they more flexible? (If the direct action appears to oppose or challenge some basic doctrine or teaching of the Church, you can expect the resistance to be adamant.)

4. **COMMUNICATIONS:** How effective are power-holders likely to be in getting their message out to Catholics and the public at large? How will they do this? What is their relationship to the mass media? Are they likely to find support through favorable editorials, articles, and commentaries?

5. **STRATEGIES:** What is the level of their strategic skill? What strategies and tactics are they likely to use in response to our challenge?

6. **STRENGTHS AND WEAKNESSES:** Where are they strongest? Where are they most vulnerable? (For instance, in the mansion example, one weakness might be the difficulty of being Christian leaders while living in a residence so antithetical to Jesus' values.)

One of many Christian demonstrations against poverty organized by Sojourners.
*Photo by Ryan Rodrick Beiler, courtesy of www.sojo.net*

*LOVE IN ACTION*

# Appendix 4
# Key Elements of Effective Nonviolent Direct-Action Campaigns

The lunch counter sit-ins begun by Black students in 1960 in Greensboro, North Carolina are a classic example of successful direct action. The act of sitting in showed the determination of Black people to have equal service. It undercut the myth that they were "happy" with segregation. White segregationists' fierce negative reaction brought to the surface the violence and hatred necessary to maintain a segregated status quo. It put a spotlight on an unjust situation that had been hidden in the darkness. It painted a vivid picture which didn't require a complicated explanation to get across its point.

American civil-rights activists often called this a *socio-drama,* a kind of public theater that delivers its message visually and verbally, touching the minds, hearts, and hopefully the consciences of those watching it. In his famous "Letter from the Birmingham Jail," Martin Luther King wrote that his approach "so seeks so to dramatize the issue that it can no longer be ignored . . . Injustice must be exposed."

Any effective direct-action campaign rooted in gospel nonviolence has twelve essential qualities:

1. The action is rooted in faith and prayer.

2. It educates the public by creating a socio-drama that paints a clear, stark picture of the injustice and the fallacy of the rationalizations used to cover it up.

3. It appeals to widely held values, such as justice, liberty, faith, Jesus' example, and lack of hypocrisy.

4. It is based on truth and justice—it is not being used to support an unfounded claim of supposed wrong.

5. It features a well-thought-out strategy—the direct-action group's strongest qualities are used to highlight weaknesses and vulnerabilities in power-holders.

6. It has momentum and builds toward a climax (for example, Gandhi's Salt March to the sea).

7. The participants are willing to sacrifice for what they believe.

8. The participants show creative goodwill toward all who oppose them.

9. The campaign is not just a single action—pressure is sustained over weeks, months, or even years.

10. It is direct, not indirect. It makes a straightforward assault on the injustice through persuasion, protest, noncooperation, and intervention.

11. It draws in people who see it and gives them positive ideas for how they can address the same injustice.

12. It offers a solution by which the wrong can be overcome.

# Appendix 5
# Civil Disobedience and Divine Obedience:
## Arrest, Jail, and Courts

**M**ost nonviolent direct action does not involve breaking the law and risking arrest. However, there are times when those committed to active nonviolence conclude that "We must obey God rather than any human authority" (Acts 5:29).

### WHAT IS CIVIL DISOBEDIENCE?

Because it so often involves perceived obedience to God rather than following a human law, many Christians prefer the term *divine obedience* over *civil disobedience*. Whatever we call it, this form of direct action deliberately, peacefully, and openly violates one or more laws, decrees, regulations, or police orders viewed as illegitimate in order to support a higher purpose.

### HOW CAN CHRISTIANS JUSTIFY BREAKING THE LAW?

Clearly, there are times when it is more moral to break a law than to obey it. All the anti-Jewish laws in Nazi Germany were perfectly legal, but we now praise as moral and religious heroes those who defied those laws to protect Jews. We also admire the operators of the U.S. underground railroad, even though they broke the Fugitive Slave Law. When Rosa Parks, a devout Christian, refused to give up her seat in the front of a bus to a White passenger, she was breaking Alabama law. This act of civil disobedience helped spark a powerful, nonviolent movement that abolished one hundred years of legal segregation in the American South.

Scripture describes many instances of civil disobedience. Divine obedience is portrayed in passages like Exodus 1:15–2:10, Esther 3:8, Daniel 6:1–16, and Mark 2:23–24—to mention only a few. Catholic theology also sanctions civil disobedience. The Church's official, Vatican-approved *Catechism of the Catholic Church* teaches that "the citizen is obliged in conscience not to follow the directive of civil authorities when they are contrary to the demands of the moral order, to the fundamental rights of persons, or to the teachings of the Gospel" (#2242).

## IF YOUR GROUP CONTEMPLATES CIVIL DISOBEDIENCE

If your group is exploring civil disobedience (CD), there are several steps to which you should commit. **First, encourage those thinking about CD to discern prayerfully** whether this is God's call for them. Getting arrested is serious business. No one should feel pressured.

**Second, participants need to prepare.** They should arrange for coverage of home and work responsibilities while they are away. Upon arrest, police probably will confiscate their possessions (to be returned upon release). Therefore, they should not carry anything that could be considered a weapon (even a nail file) or an illegal drug. If someone normally carries medicine, make sure they are in the original, prescription-marked containers. Otherwise, charges of illegal drug possession may be added to other charges. Those with medical conditions should be aware that their medication may not be returned to them until release from jail.

**Third, contact legal counsel for advice**—ideally an attorney sympathetic to the cause who has experience in civil-disobedience cases. Some people may choose to act as their own attorney in court and do not want a lawyer's assistance. However, sympathetic lawyers can give invaluable legal advice and support prior to and during the arrest. They can represent in court those who want legal defense and can advise about issues like bail, the implications of different pleas, and legal rights during incarceration.

**Fourth, let participants know their legal risks.** Find out what laws they are likely to be charged with breaking and what possible penalties they will face. Remember judges often have discretion to impose less than the maximum penalty, and in cases of nonviolent civil disobedience, they often do. Make clear to your group, however, that your legal research is only an educated guess. With the help of legal counsel, you can make a reasonable estimate of what may happen, but you cannot know for certain. Some key questions to research and inform your group about are: What enforcement body is most likely to do the arresting—federal, state, or local? Where is the group likely to be detained? What are the most likely legal steps from the time of arrest until the disposition of the case?

**Fifth, contact the police in the jurisdiction** of your civil disobedience site to inform them about your group's plans and its nonviolent spirit. You are not asking permission. The discussion may also give you an idea of how the police are likely to react on the day of your action. Remember that law enforcement officers may try to discourage you by overstressing the severity of possible penalties or by telling you that you cannot demonstrate at your chosen location. Be open to reasonable negotiation, but firm about your constitutional right to demonstrate nonviolently for "redress of grievances" (*Constitution of the United States*, Amendment I).

All of these uncertainties about possible penalties and police reactions can be positive if interpreted from a faith perspective. They remind us that our action is in God's hands, not ours. When we place ourselves at the mercy of the police and judicial system, we gain some appreciation of Jesus' last days.

## WHAT HAPPENS BEFORE, DURING, AND AFTER ARRESTS?

On rare occasions, no arrests take place. Police have been known to "wait out" a group until it has to leave, even though the action it carried out would normally result in arrest. In a few cases, police have transported people some distance in a bus before releasing them. Most civil disobedience, however, will result in an arrest.

Legal processes vary in different jurisdictions. In general, these are likely steps:

**1. WARNING:** In most cases, police warn demonstrators prior to arrest, announcing something like: "Leave in five minutes, or you will be arrested." Observe carefully what the police do, and write it down if possible. What you see may be valuable in court testimony later if, for example, the police claim they gave a warning, but failed to do so.

**2. ARREST:** The arresting officers probably will pat-search you and restrain you with metal or plastic handcuffs. Then they will take you (in a police van or bus) to a holding area such as a police station or a city or county jail. This is a good opportunity to practice the nonviolence of Christ by showing goodwill toward all authorities through words and body language. "Do not be afraid or terrified with fear of them," St. Peter advises, "but sanctify Christ as Lord in your hearts" (1 Peter 3:14–15).

**3. CHARGES:** The arresting officers may file a preliminary set of charges against you immediately or upon booking. For example, you may be charged with "failure to obey the lawful order of a police officer." These charges are not final, and may be changed before your arraignment in court. However, if you are working with a lawyer, he or she should be able to let you know the charges before arraignment.

**4. BOOKING AND PROCESSING:** You will be booked at the arrest site or later. Your possessions will be taken and inventoried for return after release, and you will be photographed and fingerprinted. Your name, address, occupation, and social security number will be recorded. It is unlikely, but possible, that you will be strip-searched (for drugs or weapons), your clothes taken, and jail clothes provided.

**5. JAIL:** Participants are kept in a large common holding area or in cells. The cells can be quite uncomfortable—crowded, noisy, possibly very hot or cold, with one open toilet and wash basin. You have a right to a phone call, but may not get it. You have a right to confer with a lawyer, but may not see one until arraignment. You may be offered an opportunity to cite out (leave detention after signing a form promising to appear in court later). You may be offered bond release, allowing you to leave when you put up a set amount of money and promise to appear in court. (The money might be your own, or come from a bonding agent you hire.)

**6. ARRAIGNMENT AND PLEA:** You are brought before a judge, often with other demonstrators. If you have an attorney, he or she will be there to represent you. The judge will tell you your rights, inform you of the charges against you, and ask how you plead. The three possible responses are guilty, not guilty or *nolo contendere*. (The latter "no contest" plea says that you accept the facts as alleged, but do not admit guilt and will offer no defense.) If you plead guilty, the judge will either sentence you right away or set a later sentencing date. If your plea is not guilty, the judge normally will set a trial date, then offer you bail or "release on your own recognizance" (a promise by you to appear for trial on a certain date).

**7. TRIAL:** If you plead not guilty, you will have a trial by jury or (more likely) by a judge. The prosecution has the burden of trying to prove your legal guilt. Your lawyer may defend you or the entire group. The judge may or may not give you a chance to make a statement about why you committed civil disobedience.

**8. VERDICT:** The judge or jury either acquits you or finds you guilty.

**9. SENTENCING:** If you are found guilty, the judge will either sentence you at the time of the verdict or later. Prior to sentencing, you will often be able to address the court on issues related to the case or matters that might influence sentencing. Sentences may involve jail, fines, probation, community service, or a suspended sentence. If the penalty is jail, imprisonment may begin immediately or at a date set by the judge.

An activist is arrested on the steps of the Supreme Court for an act of civil disobedience during an antitorture demonstration.
*Photo by Ben Schumin*

# SUPPORT FOR THOSE IN JAIL

It is helpful to name an individual or support committee to maintain contact with participants and accompany them through the legal process. It is reassuring for those arrested to know that friends on the outside won't let them get lost. Supporters should be in touch with the lawyers to work out the role each will play. Here are important tasks supporters can do:

1. Make a list of those arrested.

2. Find out from police or lawyers what charges are being filed, where people are being taken for holding and processing, and when the court appearance will be.

3. Let friends and family members know what is happening.

4. Organize supporters to be in the courtroom when those arrested are brought in for arraignment and sentencing.

5. Have rides waiting for people when they are released.

6. If bail is needed or fines imposed, raise money for a bail fund to help with these costs.

7. Don't forget the person's friends, work colleagues, and family. They may face hardships—or at least major inconveniences—in scheduling, covering added responsibilities, or caring for children. They will be worried about those arrested. Organize support for them as well, including childcare, financial help, and emotional and spiritual care.

# THE CLOUD OF WITNESSES

When we act on the conviction that divine obedience sometimes requires civil disobedience, we join hands with Christian witnesses over the centuries. Tens of thousands of believers, named and unnamed, have trod this path before us. They follow in the steps of Jesus himself.

The witnesses of many of these powerful souls of faith are found throughout these pages. Their testimonies serve as practical models of strategy as well as inspiration. This book is dedicated to all people, before and to come, who courageously choose to obey the commands of God rather than human laws. May their wisdom and discernment join your own as you pray to do what is necessary to live faithful to the gospel.

# About the Author

Over the past fifty years, Richard Taylor has led or participated in hundreds of demonstrations for peace and justice. Drawing on that experience, he has written five books, five training manuals, and over ninety articles.

Dick marched with Dr. Martin Luther King Jr. in Selma, Alabama, and served as one of Dr. King's field staff during the civil rights movement. In later decades, he co-founded several nonviolent social change organizations, including the St. Vincent's Peace Center, American Christians for the Abolition of Torture, and Witness for Peace. He also organized and led Project FREE (For Real Estate Equality), a nonviolent movement to combat racial discrimination in housing.

In the early 1970s, Dick worked with other nonviolent activists to challenge U.S. support for a brutal West Pakistani dictatorship that slaughtered thousands of people in what was then East Pakistan. A primary tactic was to use canoes to block Pakistani ships from entering U.S. harbors to receive U.S. military aid. The resulting world-wide publicity helped stop the aid and was instrumental in creating out of East Pakistan the new nation of Bangladesh. Several Bangladeshi organizations have honored Dick and his wife Phyllis, calling them "courageous soldiers for human rights, armed with nonviolence and love for humanity."

Dick grew up as a Quaker and worked with Quakers for two years in El Salvador, after which he studied for a year at Yale Divinity School as a Rockefeller Fellow, then received his masters' degree from Bryn Mawr School of Social Work. Dick joined the Catholic Church in 1982 at forty-nine years of age.

Currently, Dick is coordinator of ministry development at St. Vincent de Paul Catholic Church in Philadelphia. He has written about his belief in the fundamental goodness, truth, and beauty of the Catholic Church in an article, "Why I Am Still Catholic," in an issue of the *National Catholic Reporter.*

Dick's wife Phyllis is a nonviolence trainer and activist, as well as a prison reformer, human-rights advocate, and hospice-care pioneer. They have been married for forty-four years and have three children and nine grandchildren. They live in Philadelphia.

# Acknowledgments

Profound thanks to my beloved wife, Phyllis, for putting up with late nights and husband preoccupation, intensity, and maddening perfectionism during the months of writing this handbook. Thanks also to Dee Dee Risher for her careful editing, helpful suggestions, and publishing advice and to Ellen Moore Osborne for her creative work on artistic design. And thanks to Aimee Carevich Hariramani, whose encouragement led me to write the manual in the first place and whose suggestions improved it immensely.

Breinigsville, PA USA
23 June 2010
240398BV00001B/1/P